Creation of the Modern Middle East

Jordan

Creation of the Modern Middle East

Jordan

Hal Marcovitz

Introduction by
Akbar Ahmed
School of International Service
American University

CHELSEA HOUSE
P U B L I S H E R S
A Haights Cross Communications ✦ Company
Philadelphia

Frontispiece: **Huwaytat Sheik, 1912**
This is a rare photograph of a Huwaytat sheik (center) on his white stallion. The armed horseman to the left was the sheik's protector, and the one to the right was the sheik's servant. The Huwaytat were then among the largest nomadic Bedouin groups in what is present-day Jordan.

CHELSEA HOUSE PUBLISHERS

VP, NEW PRODUCT DEVELOPMENT Sally Cheney
DIRECTOR OF PRODUCTION Kim Shinners
CREATIVE MANAGER Takeshi Takahashi
MANUFACTURING MANAGER Diann Grasse

Staff for JORDAN

EDITOR Lee Marcott
PRODUCTION EDITOR Jaimie Winkler
PICTURE RESEARCHER Sarah Bloom
COVER AND SERIES DESIGNER Keith Trego
LAYOUT 21st Century Publishing and Communications, Inc.

A Haights Cross Communications ✈ Company

http://www.chelseahouse.com

First Printing

1 3 5 7 9 8 6 4 2

Library of Congress Cataloging-in-Publication Data

Marcovitz, Hal.
 Jordan / Hal Marcovitz.
   p. cm. -- (Creation of the modern Middle East)
Summary: A history of the nation of Jordan and a discussion of its role in the Middle East.
Includes bibliographical references and index.
 ISBN 0-7910-6507-3
 1. Jordan--History--1946-1952. 2. Jordan--History--1952-1999. 3. Jordan--History--1999- [1. Jordan.] I. Title. II. Series.
 DS154.53 .M37 2002
 956.9504'3--dc21
                                    2002009600

Table of Contents

Index to the Photographs

Creation of the Modern Middle East

Iran

Iraq

Israel

Jordan

The Kurds

Kuwait

Oman

Palestinian Authority

Saudi Arabia

Syria

Turkey

Yemen

Introduction

Akbar Ahmed

The Middle East, it seems, is always in the news. Unfortunately, most of the news is of a troubling kind. Stories of suicide bombers, hijackers, street demonstrations, and ongoing violent conflict dominate these reports. The conflict draws in people living in lands far from the Middle East; some support one group, some support another, often on the basis of kinship or affinity and not on the merits of the case.

The Middle East is often identified with the Arabs. The region is seen as peopled by Arabs speaking Arabic and belonging to the Islamic faith. The stereotype of the Arab oil sheikh is a part of contemporary culture. But both of these images—that the Middle East is in perpetual anarchy and that it has an exclusive Arab identity—are oversimplifications of the region's complex contemporary reality.

In reality, the Middle East is an area that straddles Africa and Asia and has a combined population of over 200 million people inhabiting over twenty countries. It is a region that draws the entire world into its politics and, above all, it is the land that is the birth place of the three great Abrahamic faiths—Judaism, Christianity, and Islam. The city of Jerusalem is the point at which these three faiths come together and also where they tragically confront one another.

It is for these reasons that knowledge of the Middle East will remain of importance and that news from it will remain ongoing and interesting.

Let us consider the stereotype of the Middle East as a land of constant anarchy. It is easy to forget that some of the greatest lawgivers and people of peace were born, lived, and died here. In the Abrahamic tradition these names are a glorious roll call of human history—Abraham, Moses, Jesus, and Muhammad. In the tradition of the Middle East, where these names are especially revered, people often add the blessing "Peace be upon him" when speaking their names.

The land is clearly one that is shared by the great faiths. While it has a dominant Muslim character because of the large Muslim population, its Jewish and Christian presence must not be underestimated. Indeed, it is the dynamics of the relationships between the three faiths that allow us to enter the Middle East today and appreciate the points where these faiths come together or are in conflict.

To understand the predicament in which the people of the Middle East find themselves today, it is well to keep the facts of history before us. History is never far from the minds of the people in this region. Memories of the first great Arab dynasty, the Umayyads (661-750), based in Damascus, and the even greater one of the Abbasids (750-1258), based in Baghdad, are still kept alive in books and folklore. For the Arabs, their history, their culture, their tradition, their language, and above all their religion, provide them with a rich source of pride; but the glory of the past contrasts with the reality and powerlessness of contemporary life.

Many Arabs have blamed past rulers for their current situation beginning with the Ottomans who ruled them until World War I and then the European powers that divided their lands. When they achieved independence after World War II they discovered that the artificial boundaries created by the European powers cut across tribes and clans. Today, too, they complain that a form of Western imperialism still dominates their politics and rulers.

Again, while it is true that Arab history and Arab temperament have colored the Middle East strongly, there are other distinct peoples who have made a significant contribution to the culture of the region. Turkey is one such non-Arab nation with its own language, culture, and contribution to the region through the influence of the Ottoman Empire. Memories of that period for the Arabs are mixed, but what cannot be denied are the spectacular administrative and architectural achievements of the Ottomans. It is the longest dynasty in world history, beginning in 1300 and ending after World War I in 1922, when Kemal Ataturk wished to reject the past on the way to creating a modern Turkey.

Similarly, Iran is another non-Arab country with its own rich language and culture. Based in the minority sect of Islam, the Shia, Iran has often been in opposition to its Sunni neighbors, both Arab and Turk. Perhaps this confrontation helped to forge a unique Iranian, or Persian, cultural identity that, in turn, created the brilliant art, architecture, and poetry under the Safawids (1501-1722). The Safawid period also saw the establishment of the principle of interference or participation—depending on one's perspective—in matters of the state by the religious clerics. So while the Ayatollah Khomeini was very much a late 20th century figure, he was nonetheless reflecting the patterns of Iranian history.

Israel, too, represents an ancient, non-Arabic, cultural and religious tradition. Indeed, its very name is linked to the tribes that figure prominently in the stories of the Bible and it is through Jewish tradition that memory of the great biblical patriarchs like Abraham and Moses is kept alive. History is not a matter of years, but of millennia, in the Middle East.

Perhaps nothing has evoked as much emotional and political controversy among the Arabs as the creation of the state of Israel in 1948. With it came ideas of democracy and modern culture that seemed alien to many Arabs. Many saw the wars that followed stir further conflict and hatred; they also saw the wars as an inevitable clash between Islam and Judaism.

It is therefore important to make a comment on Islam and Judaism. The roots of prejudice against Jews can be anti-Semitic, anti-Judaic, and anti-Zionist. The prejudice may combine all three and there is often a degree of overlap. But in the case of the Arabs, the matter is more complicated because, by definition, Arabs cannot be anti-Semitic because they themselves are considered Semites. They cannot be anti-Judaic, because Islam recognizes the Jews as "people of the Book."

What this leaves us with is the clash between the political philosophy of Zionism, which is the establishment of a Jewish nation in Palestine, and Arab thought. The antagonism of the Arabs to Israel may result in the blurring of lines. A way must be found by Arabs and Israelis to live side by side in peace. Perhaps recognition of the common Abrahamic tradition is one way forward.

The hostility to Israel partly explains the negative coverage the Arabs get in the Western media. Arab Muslims are often accused of being anarchic and barbaric due to the violence of the Middle East. Yet, their history has produced some of the greatest figures in history.

Consider the example of Sultan Salahuddin Ayyoubi, popularly called Saladin in Western literature. Saladin had vowed to take revenge for the bloody massacres that the Crusaders had indulged in when they took Jerusalem in 1099. According to a European eyewitness account the blood in the streets was so deep that it came up to the knees of the horsemen.

Yet, when Saladin took Jerusalem in 1187, he showed the essential compassion and tolerance that is at the heart of the Abrahamic faiths. He not only released the prisoners after ransom, as was the custom, but paid for those who were too poor to afford any ransom. His nobles and commanders were furious that he had not taken a bloody revenge. Saladin is still remembered in the bazaars and villages as a leader of great learning and compassion. When contemporary leaders are compared to Saladin, they are usually found wanting. One reason may be that the problems of the region are daunting.

The Middle East faces three major problems that will need solutions in the twenty-first century. These problems affect society and politics and need to be tackled by the rulers in those lands and all other people interested in creating a degree of dialogue and participation.

The first of the problems is that of democracy. Although democracy is practiced in some form in a number of the Arab countries, for the majority of ordinary people there is little sense of participation in their government. The frustration of helplessness in the face of an indifferent bureaucracy at the lower levels of administration is easily converted to violence. The indifference of the state to the pressing needs of the "street" means that other non-governmental organizations can step in. Islamic organizations offering health and education programs to people in the shantytowns and villages have therefore emerged and flourished over the last decades.

The lack of democracy also means that the ruler becomes remote and autocratic over time as he consolidates his power. It is not uncommon for many rulers in the Middle East to pass on their rule to their son. Dynastic rule, whether kingly or based in a dictatorship, excludes ordinary people from a sense of participation in their own governance. They need to feel empowered. Muslims need to feel that they are able to participate in the process of government. They must feel that they are able to elect their leaders into office and if these leaders do not deliver on their promises, that they can throw them out. Too many of the rulers are nasty and brutish. Too many Muslim leaders are kings and military dictators. Many of them ensure that their sons or relatives stay on to perpetuate their dynastic rule.

With democracy, Muslim peoples will be able to better bridge the gaps that are widening between the rich and the poor. The sight of palatial mansions with security guards carrying automatic weapons standing outside them and, alongside, hovels teeming with starkly poor children is a common one in Muslim cities. The distribution of wealth must remain a priority of any democratic government.

The second problem in the Middle East that has wide ramifications in society is that of education. Although Islam emphasizes knowledge and learning, the sad reality is that the standards of education are unsatisfactory. In addition, the climate for scholarship and intellectual activity is discouraging. Scholars are too often silenced, jailed, or chased out of the country by the administration. The sycophants and the intelligence services whose only aim is to tell the ruler what he would like to hear, fill the vacuum.

Education needs to be vigorously reformed. The *madrassah,* or religious school, which is the institution that provides primary education for millions of boys in the Middle East, needs to be brought into line with the more prestigious Westernized schools reserved for the elite of the land. By allowing two distinct streams of education to develop, Muslim nations are encouraging the growth of two separate societies: a largely illiterate and frustrated population that is susceptible to leaders with simple answers to the world's problems and a small, Westernized, often corrupt and usually uncaring group of elite. The third problem facing the Middle East is that of representation in the mass media. Although this point is hard to pin down, the images in the media are creating problems of understanding and communication in the communities living in the Middle East. Muslims, for example, will always complain that they are depicted in negative stereotypes in the non-Arab media. The result of the media onslaught that plagues Muslims is the sense of anger on the one hand and the feeling of loss of dignity on the other. Few Muslims will discuss the media rationally. Greater Muslim participation in the media and greater interaction will help to solve the problem. But it is not so simple. The Israelis also complain of the stereotypes in the Arab media that depict them negatively.

Muslims are aware that their religious culture represents a civilization rich in compassion and tolerance. They are aware that given a period of stability in which they can grapple with the problems of democracy, education, and self-image they can take their rightful place in the community of nations. However painful the current reality, they do carry an idea of an ideal human society with them. Whether a Turk, or an Iranian, or an Arab, every Muslim is aware of the message that the prophet of Islam brought to this region in the seventh century. This message still has resonance for these societies. Here are words from the last address of the prophet spoken to his people:

> All of you descend from Adam and Adam was made of earth. There is no superiority for an Arab over a non-Arab nor for a non-Arab over an Arab, neither for a white man over a black man nor a black man over a white man . . . the noblest among you is the one who is most deeply conscious of God.

This is a noble and worthy message for the twenty-first century in the Middle East. Not only Muslims, but Jews, and Christians would agree with it. Perhaps its essential theme of tolerance, compassion, and equality can help to rediscover the wellsprings of tradition that can both inspire and unite.

It is for these reasons that I congratulate Chelsea House Publishers for taking the initiative in helping us to understand the Middle East through this series. The story of the Middle East is, in many profound ways, the story of human civilization.

— **Dr. Akbar S. Ahmed**
The Ibn Khaldun Chair of Islamic Studies and
Professor of International Relations,
School of International Service
American University

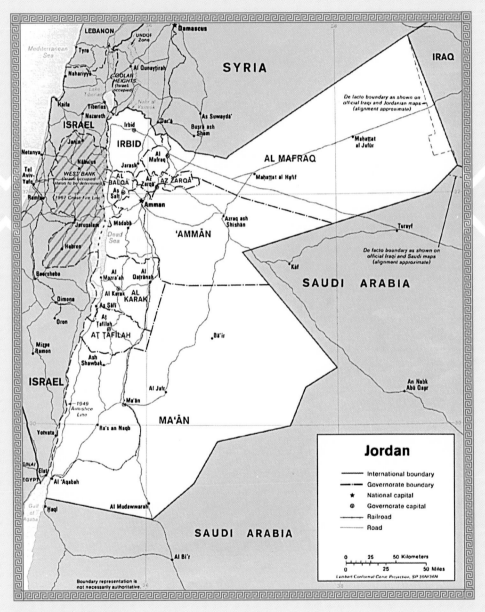

Modern Map of Jordan

King Hussein of Jordan, c. 1952

Hussein was his grandfather's favorite of all his sons and grandsons and was selected to be his successor when he was only 15 years old. This picture was taken on his 17th birthday, shortly before he ascended the throne.

1

Land of Assassins

The young king enjoyed adventure. He flew airplanes, skied down dangerous Alpine slopes, fenced with the Arab sword known as the scimitar and was an avid skydiver. One day he raced his expensive Mercedes-Benz sports car along an airport runway, reaching speeds of 150 miles per hour. "I think she could have done better, but the runway isn't quite long enough," he told friends.

The 23-year-old king also took his role as head of his country's army very seriously. Hussein ibn Talal had no reservations about donning a soldier's uniform, strapping a sidearm to his hip, and traipsing into the field to mingle with the front-line troops of Jordan's army. The soldiers in Jordan's elite British-trained Arab

Legion, the toughest fighting force in the Middle East, respected Hussein and pledged their loyalty to him.

Alas, for the young king the opportunities to race a sports car or escape to a ski slope were coming to be fewer and fewer. His country was at the center of escalating hostilities in the Middle East; indeed, the unsettled political climate in 1958 required the king not only devote himself to matters of state, but also to be wary of assassination attempts by fierce enemies who aimed to undermine his regime.

Assassination has seemed to be a way of life in the Middle East. Over the centuries, few leaders of the Arab states have been able to rule without keeping an eye focused on their enemies. In the Middle East, countless rulers—whether they assumed their thrones through royal succession, seized power through revolution, or headed their governments by way of popular elections—have fallen victim to assassination. In fact, the original "assassins" were members of an 11th-century Iranian sect that ambushed political leaders from their mountain hideouts.

King Hussein ascended the throne after his beloved grandfather, King Abdullah, was murdered on July 20, 1951, by an assassin while arriving at a mosque in Jerusalem to pray. Abdullah had three wives and many children and grandsons; he could have picked any one of them as crown prince. But Hussein was clearly his favorite, and Abdullah selected him as the successor to the throne. "He is the elite of the elite," said Abdullah. "He is the continuity of my dynasty."

Hussein, at the time just 15 years old, accompanied his grandfather to the mosque that day. When Abdullah and Hussein departed the capital city of Amman for Jerusalem, they had been well advised of the murder plot by Western diplomats as well as members of their own government. Still, Abdullah brushed off the warnings, believing he would be protected by the Islamic god Allah.

King Abdullah

On July 20, 1951, King Abdullah was assassinated by a Palestinian refugee living in a camp on the West Bank of the Jordan River. When Abdullah signed a peace treaty with the Israelis after the war in 1948, he became an enemy to many Palestinians.

The promise of Allah's protection wasn't good enough for other members of the king's traveling party. Aware of the plot, they declined to accompany the king to Jerusalem. "They were afraid," Abdullah said. "When I have to die, I should like to be shot in the head by a nobody. That's the simplest way of dying. I would rather that than become old and a burden."

Abdullah asked his grandson whether he, too, preferred

Street Scene, Amman, 1893

Today, Amman is the capital of Jordan. As of 2000, its population was estimated at more than 2 million people, about 40 percent of the country's total population.

to stay in the safety of the capital. Hussein answered that his place was by his grandfather's side: "You know, Sir, my life is worth nothing compared to yours," he said.

Hussein's reply must have pleased Abdullah, who had once told his grandson, "My boy, I want you to come always to me and try to learn what you can from what you witness at my palace. Who knows? The time may come when you will replace me on the throne."

Shortly before noon the king and his grandson arrived at the Dome of the Rock, one of the holiest sites in the Islamic world. At his grandfather's insistence, Hussein wore the uniform of the Jordanian army, in which he served as a captain. The streets leading up to the mosque were patrolled by troops, and the mosque itself was surrounded by Abdullah's bodyguards. The king's limousine pulled up to the mosque entrance; Abdullah and Hussein stepped out of the car and walked slowly into the ancient house of worship.

Just as Abdullah crossed the threshold into the mosque a man appeared from behind a pillar. He pointed a gun at the king and fired, hitting Abdullah in the head. The 69-year-old monarch died instantly. The crown prince stood frozen, shocked by the sight of his grandfather cut down by a bullet. He looked up to see the assassin pointing the gun at him. The killer fired off a shot and Hussein felt a thud against his chest, which knocked the prince backward. Hussein was stunned but not hurt; the bullet struck a medal pinned to his uniform shirt over his heart. As for the assassin, he was cut down in a fusillade of bullets fired by the king's bodyguards.

The killer turned out to be a Palestinian refugee who had been forced to live in a camp on the West Bank of the Jordan River following the Israeli War of Independence in 1948, which had erupted just after the tiny Jewish nation received recognition by the United Nations. The outnumbered Israelis had managed in a few short months to drive back the invading armies of five Arab nations. When the war ended, some 500,000 Palestinians fled to the West Bank, where they lived in camps under the protection of King Abdullah. But Abdullah became an enemy to them when he signed a peace treaty with the Israelis.

A short time after Abdullah's murder, after Hussein's

The Citadel, Amman, 1924
Jabal al-Qal'a, or citadel, the center of ancient and modern Amman, rises some 2800 feet. Although archaeological digs continue to uncover new evidence of settlement from earliest times up to the recent past, the remains here are mainly Roman, Byzantine, and early Islamic.

own father, Talal, was deposed and sent into exile, Hussein would be crowned king of Jordan.

As hostilities in the Middle East increased, so did the attempts on Hussein's life. Some of the attempts were quite bizarre. On one occasion, a palace cook tried to poison him; the plot was uncovered after aides found dead cats in the palace—the cook had tested the poison on the animals first. On another occasion, acid was placed in a container of the

The Citadel, Amman, 1924

king's nose drops. When the king spilled the drops into his bathroom sink, he was alarmed to watch the chrome that covered the drain opening form into bubbles. Later, when the king was on a visit to the United States, word reached him that 13 army officers had been arrested in Amman for planning a coup d'etat. On another occasion, a library in Amman that the king planned to visit blew up before he arrived—the bomb had been planted by two Palestinians.

In 1957, King Hussein foiled a plot to overthrow his regime led by the commander of the Jordanian army, General Ali abu Nuwar. Under orders from abu Nuwar, a division of Jordanian troops mobilized near Amman with orders to capture the king. But senior army officers, fond of the king and suspicious of abu Nuwar, informed Hussein of the plot. Hussein thwarted the coup attempt by having abu Nuwar accompany him to an army camp in the town of Zerqa, where he knew he could find loyal troops. The king strode into the ranks of men; the loyal soldiers gathered around Hussein to shake his hand and pledge their allegiance to him.

"Abu Nuwar was trembling with fright," the king recalled.

The king had the general and the other plotters kicked out of the country.

Sometimes, it seemed as though the king was likely to bring on his own death. When he could find time away from his official duties, Hussein still loved racing cars and flying planes. And in pursuing those pastimes, the king seemed fearless. Once, the front wheel of his airplane refused to lock into place as he approached the airport in Amman for a landing. After several nervous minutes, Hussein jolted the landing gear into place by exploding a bottle of compressed air just over the wheel. The plane landed safely.

"All this worry about my flying is silly," he told friends on the ground. "I've taken off from the desert at night by the lights of automobile head lamps. I've flown with over-weight loads and in all kinds of weather. Flying is safe enough for anyone with a good head and a good aircraft."

Meanwhile, as Hussein continually found himself dodging assassination attempts that originated inside Jordan, his relationships with other Arab leaders were testy as well. In February 1958, Gamal Abdel Nasser, the president of Egypt, signed a pact with Syrian leaders, agreeing to unite their countries in a federation they called the United Arab Republic. Nasser was a virulently nationalistic leader—he dreamed of a single Arab empire composed of the many Middle Eastern states, and the UAR was clearly the first step toward that goal. However, although they were now members of the same federation, Egypt and Syria were not contiguous neighbors. They were separated geographically by Jordan and Israel.

Hussein realized the intentions of Nasser: to invade Jordan, overthrow his regime, and force the country to become part of the UAR. With Jordan part of the federation, Nasser's next objective would be to cross the Jordan River and destroy Israel.

Egypt was clearly the dominant member of the UAR. The Egyptian army was the largest in the Middle East. It was also well-armed; Nasser maintained a friendship with the former Soviet Union, and could rely on the one-time superpower to provide his nation and its allies with tanks, jets, and other sophisticated weapons.

To protect his country, Hussein signed a mutual aid pact with Iraq, which was ruled by his cousin Faisal. Iraq saw itself as the next victim of Egyptian aggression. The two countries agreed to face the Egyptian-Syrian threat together. Nevertheless, Hussein and his allies in Iraq knew their partnership, which they called the Arab Federation, was no match for the far superior UAR forces.

Still, Hussein felt confident enough in his regime that year to plan a holiday in Geneva, Switzerland—location of some of the best ski slopes in the world. He sent his family on ahead and planned to join them by flying his own plane to Switzerland. To make the trip, Hussein selected a British-made De Havilland Dove, a small twin-engine passenger plane that was very fast and very maneuverable—exactly the type of plane the king enjoyed flying.

Hussein and his copilot, Jock Dalgleish, left the airport in Amman the afternoon of November 10, 1958. Dalgleish was a high-ranking officer in the Jordanian air force and a long-time friend of the king; shortly after Abdullah's murder, Dalgleish became Hussein's bodyguard, protecting the boy in the frantic first few hours after his grandfather's death. Hussein's uncle, Sharif Nasser bin Jamil, also accompanied the king on the flight. Their intent was to fly first to the island of Cyprus in the eastern Meditteranean to refuel, then head north for Geneva. To reach Cyprus, Hussein needed to fly over Syrian territory.

Later, Hussein would claim that Syrian leaders had been made aware of his plans and had granted permission for the flight. Once over Syria, though, the king was advised by the control tower at the airport in the capital of Damascus that he did not have clearance and should land at the nearest Syrian air field. It became obvious to Hussein what the Syrians had in mind: once the De Havilland Dove landed, he would be taken prisoner.

Suddenly, two Syrian air force jets appeared to the south of the De Havilland. (The jets, called MiGs, had been provided to the UAR by the Soviet Union; the name is derived from the initials of the plane's Russian designers— Mikoyan and Gurevich.) The MiGs were much faster than Hussein's propeller-driven plane, and within seconds they overtook the De Havilland.

For the next several minutes Hussein and Dalgleish wrestled with the controls of the De Havilland, working feverishly to escape from the MiGs. Certainly, either of the MiGs could have shot the unarmed De Havilland down with just a few bursts from its machine guns, but the Syrian pilots seemed to have no interest in shooting down the king's plane. Instead, Hussein realized, the MiGs were trying to force his plane to land or crash into the desert floor—to make it look like an accident. The two jets zoomed past the nose of the tiny plane from opposite directions, each time narrowly missing the De Havilland.

Hussein threw the De Havilland into a power dive and headed straight to the ground. It was a clever but dangerous evasive maneuver. Had the jets followed him down they never would have been able to pull out of their dives before crashing into the desert. But the little De Havilland came out of the power dive nicely; Hussein turned the plane south and, flying very low to the ground, zigzagged his way back to Amman.

Later, he learned that some 200 of his Jordanian opponents had gathered at the airport in Damascus at the invitation of Syrian leaders, who obviously had planned a hostile welcome for a captive Jordanian king. But it didn't work out that way. Once again, King Hussein of Jordan had survived an attempt on his life.

Bedouins, 1910

This photograph of Jordanian Bedouins was a posed scene that was sold commercially to tourists throughout the Middle East.

Tourism to the Middle East expanded enormously after the opening of the Suez Canal in 1869. Many came on their way to India. The travel agency Thomas Cook & Son opened in a Cairo office in the 1870s, and by 1905 the company had a "tourist camp" at Petra that was frequented by a steady trickle of privileged sight-seers. At this point, photography was still in its infancy, but several photographers realized the financial potential of combining their skill with this surge in tourism. Local views and posed studio photographs were mounted on stiff cardboard and sold wherever tourists congregated.

2
Transjordan

When Winston Churchill arrived in Cairo, Egypt, in March 1921, he was faced with the rather thorny job of fulfilling conflicting promises Great Britain had made to two groups of people not known for their love of one another: Jews and Arabs.

In 1917, the British government had adopted the "Balfour Declaration" supporting the desire of Jews to establish a homeland in Palestine, the traditional homeland of Jews since the days of the Hebrew kings. Chaim Weizmann, an English Jew and noted scientist, had lobbied the British government for years to support such a declaration. Finally, British foreign secretary Arthur James Balfour issued the statement, saying: "His Majesty's government views with favor the establishment in Palestine of a national home for the Jewish people and will use their best efforts to facilitate the achievement of this object, it being clearly understood that nothing shall be done which may prejudice the civil and religious rights of existing non-Jewish communities in Palestine or the rights and political status enjoyed by Jews in any other country."

Five years later, the League of Nations—a forerunner of the United Nations—adopted the "British Mandate," giving the British authority over Palestine until they regarded Palestine ready to govern itself. The League of Nations incorporated the Balfour Declaration into the mandate, meaning the British were to pursue the creation of a Jewish homeland.

There were more reasons for the Balfour Declaration than simply Great Britain's desire to appease Chaim Weizmann. At the time, Britain found itself fighting Germany and the other so-called Central Powers virtually alone in World War I. France was Britain's major ally in the war, but the French people had been worn down by some three years of fighting, most of which was on French land. The Balfour Declaration was issued because the British believed America had an influential Jewish community; it was hoped Jews in America would pressure their government's leaders to join Britain in the war.

The United States eventually did enter the war, but not because of the Balfour Declaration. German submarine attacks on American shipping prompted President Woodrow Wilson to declare war on the Central Powers. Nevertheless, when the war ended in 1918 the Jews of Palestine expected Great Britain to support their independence.

While Great Britain had made promises to the Jews, it had also made promises to the Arabs. In 1916, prompted by the British, Arab leaders had staged the Great Arab Revolt against the Ottoman Turks, who were allied with the

Central Powers. For nearly 500 years the Arabs had seethed under the Turkish sultans, who had expanded their empire into the Middle East in the 16th century. This empire included Egypt, Syria, and Arabia. Mecca—the holiest city in the Islamic world—was under the authority of the hated Turks.

By the early 1900s, though, the influence and power of the Ottoman Turks was very much on the wane. The once-powerful Turkish empire was now regarded as the "Sick Man of Europe," suffering from poverty at home, poor training for soldiers, and laziness by their leaders who were more interested in fattening their own fortunes than in defending the Ottomans' vast foreign holdings. What's more, the sultans had to contend with revolution in their capital of Constantinople. During the first years of the 20th century, the powers of the Ottoman sultans had eroded to the point where they no longer could count on the loyalty of their troops.

And so in 1916, Great Britain realized it had the opportunity to drive the Turks out of the war by encouraging the Arabs to rise up against their long-hated oppressors. In return, the British promised to restore their kingdoms following the war. Indeed, the Arabs fought bravely against the Turks. They were led by British army officer T. E. Lawrence, a swashbuckling adventurer dispatched by his government to serve as a military adviser.

But once the war was over, the British found themselves facing not only the demands of the Arabs and the Jews, but their own self-interests as well. Even in the early years of the 20th century, the Middle East was recognized as the source of tremendous oil reserves. As industry in the Western nations began relying more and more on the gasoline-fueled internal combustion engine, political leaders realized a guaranteed source of oil would be vital to their countries' economies. Britain, which also desired a guaranteed source of

Inauguration of the Haifa–Dar'a (Deraa) Branch of the Hejaz Railroad, Dar'a (Deraa), 1905

The Hejaz Railroad (constructed between 1900 and 1908) was one of the principal railroads of the Ottoman Empire. Its main line was from Damascus southward. It entered what is now Jordan at Dar'a (Deraa) and then, via Ma'an, into north-western Arabia and on to Medina. A major branch line, about 100 miles long, from Dar'a (Deraa) to Haifa on the Mediterranean coast, was completed in 1905. This photograph is of the commemorative ceremonies marking the completion of that branch line.

　　The purpose of the railroad, which was supervised by German engineers, was to facilitate pilgrimages to the Muslim holy places in Arabia. It also strengthened Ottoman control over the most distant provinces of the empire.

Railroad Bridge, Ma'an, 1908

This Hejaz Railroad bridge at Ma'an was mainly destroyed in 1917 by Arab guerrillas led by their English leader T. E. Lawrence ("Lawrence of Arabia"). This raid effectively stopped railroad traffic from Ma'an to Medina. Plans to restore this part of the railroad have never been fulfilled.

oil for its navy, aimed to control those oil reserves. And so did France, which had emerged from the war with its industries shattered and its people destitute but, nevertheless, on the winning side.

The strategic importance of the Middle East to Britain as well as to other world powers also went beyond oil interests. Armies stationed in the Middle East could easily be sent to trouble spots in Europe to the north, Africa to the south, and Asia to the east.

The land at the hub of this valuable region was territory in western Arabia that was rocky, untillable, and mountainous; it was a land separating the two great Middle East capitals of Cairo and Damascus, occupied mostly by nomadic Bedouin tribesmen because no one else wanted to live there. On the map, this land could be found along the east bank of the Jordan River—the land of Palestine.

The first settlements were established along the Jordan River some 5,000 years ago. The Shasu, early nomadic tribesmen, were among the first settlers. By 1500 B.C., the land was part of Canaan, the territory conquered by the Egyptians that now includes Israel, Jordan, and Syria. According to the Bible, it was at about this time that the Jews were freed from bondage in Egypt by Moses and wandered in the desert for 40 years before finding their homeland across the Jordan River. Just before crossing the river they stopped so Moses could ascend Mount Nebo in Jordan, where he died. The Israelite leader Joshua then led the Jews across the river to Palestine. The Jews built a kingdom across the river, where they were led by the kings Saul, David, and Solomon.

Over the next several centuries the land was ruled by a series of conquering peoples—the Assyrians, Babylonians, Persians, Greeks, and Romans among them. In the year 333 A.D. the emperor Constantine expanded the reach of Christianity in the region. Nearly 300 years later, a merchant named Muhammad ibn Abdullah claimed to have heard the word of God, and the Arab world was changed forever.

Known as the Prophet, Muhammad at first led a normal and quite unremarkable life in the Arabian city of

Bedouins, near Fassua, 1912

The Bedouins are an Arabic-speaking nomadic people who live in the Middle Eastern deserts, especially those of Arabia, Iraq, Syria, and Jordan.

At the end of World War I (1914–18), the Bedouin tribes had to submit to the control of the new national governments in which their wandering areas lay.

Today, it is estimated that Bedouins make up less than one-tenth of the Jordanian population.

Mecca. He was born in about the year 570 A.D., a member of the Hashem clan. He married at 25, taking for his wife Khadija bint Khuwaylid, a rich widow 15 years his senior. When he was 40, Muhammad started having visions of supernatural beings. One of those beings was the angel Gabriel, who told Muhammad, "Recite! You are the Messenger of God!"

God, known to Muslims as Allah, then commanded Muhammad to repeat his words, which came to be

Roman Theater, Amman, 1893

Philadelphia was the ancient Greek and Roman name for present-day Amman. Philadelphia's best-preserved monument is this theater, mostly built into the hillside. It was constructed between 169 and 177 A.D. during the reign of Marcus Aurelius and could seat about 6000. Selah Merrill, archaeologist of the American Palestine Exploration Society, who visited Amman in 1876–77, noted that the theater was in a sorry state: "I spent a part of one night in the great theatre, when the moon was shining with all its intensity. The sense of desolation was oppressive. Kings, princes, wealth and beauty once came here to be entertained, where now I see only piles of stones, owls and bats, wretched fellahin and donkeys, goats and filth."

Today, the building has been restored. The theater, with its excellent acoustics, is once more used for performances.

known as the Koran—the set of laws that govern the Islamic faith. It took several years for Muhammad to recite the laws. His words were recorded on scraps of leather, flat stone tablets, even camel bones.

In English, Islam means "submission to God." Believers in this religion accept five basic laws: the *shahada*—the tenet that there is one god, Allah, and one messenger, Muhammad; the *salat*—the duty to pray five times a day;

the celebration of Ramadan, the holy month in which it is necessary to fast from sunrise to sunset; *zakat*—the notion of donating to charity; and, finally, making at least one pilgrimage in one's lifetime to Mecca, the birthplace of the new religion.

At first, Arabs in Mecca and elsewhere refused to accept the new religion. Many of them worshiped multiple deities and they rejected the idea of one supreme being. Slowly, though, the Arab people began converting. Most of the early followers were drawn to Islam by the personal appeal of Muhammad, an enormously persuasive and charismatic leader who seemed to possess a gift for resolving disputes. Others joined Islam after they were conquered by Muslim armies. Unlike the first Christians, who were taught to "turn the other cheek," the Muslims were prepared to fight to spread the word of the Prophet.

Soon, the Muslims under Muhammad had conquered cities in the Arab world. In 632 A.D., the much-beloved Prophet died. His first successor was Abu Bakr, who was installed by Muslim leaders in Mecca as the first *caliph*, which means "successor." Under Abu Bakr the Muslims became a formidable military force and their influence spread throughout the Arab world. After Abu Bakr, though, the Muslim people would find themselves falling victim to the jealousy, ambition, and violence that would haunt their leaders into the 21st century. The third caliph, Umar, was assassinated by a non-Muslim. Umar's successor, Uthman, was killed by dissident Muslims enraged at his selection as caliph. For the first time, a Muslim leader was murdered by fellow Muslims.

Nevertheless, the religion continued to grow and along with it the Middle East itself. The great Middle Eastern cities of Damascus, Alexandria, Beirut, Jerusalem, Baghdad, and Cairo became important trading centers. For some 300 years, the Christian armies of Western

Arabs, al Karak, 1921

Al Karak is in west-central Jordan, about 15 miles east of the Dead Sea. It has been continuously inhabited since ancient times. This site is one of the capitals of the Moabs in the Old Testament.

The town, with a population of 50,000 (2000 est.), contains evidence of virtually all the peoples who lived in this area, including the ruins of several Byzantine churches and a crusader's fort. On the Ma'daba mosaic map, the oldest known map of the Holy Land and its environs (sixth century A.D.), al Karak is shown as a walled city.

Europe tried to capture the city of Jerusalem and return its holy sites to Christianity. But the Muslims proved to be too formidable a fighting force. The most fearsome Muslim warrior during those years was Saladin, whose Muslim empire stretched from the Libyan desert in North Africa to the Tigris River in Iraq.

In the late 13th century, Marco Polo traipsed through the deserts of Arabia, Syria, and Iraq on his way to China, esablishing the Middle East as an important trade route between Europe and China. The Ottoman Turks arrived 300 years later. Included in the Ottoman reign was the territory of Arabia along the Red Sea known as the Hejaz. In 1908, the Ottoman Sultan Abdul Hamid recognized Hussein ibn Ali as sharif, or prince, of the Hejaz.

Born in the Turkish capital of Constantinople in 1853, Sharif Hussein was the son of an Arab father and a Circassian mother. Circassians are non-Arab Muslims from the Caucasus region of Russia just east of Turkey. Hussein was a Hashemite, meaning he was a direct descendant of the Prophet Muhammad and, therefore, born to rule.

But of course, with the Turks the overall masters of the Arab world, Sharif Hussein could merely oversee the rocky strip of land of the Hejaz and even there his authority was limited. Still, Hussein knew the hand of the Turks was slipping.

Sharif Hussein had four sons: Faisal, Abdullah, Zeid, and Ali. The boys were educated in the cosmopolitan city of Constantinople; when they returned, Hussein sent them into the desert to learn the Arab ways. "Soon they hardened and became self-reliant," wrote T. E. Lawrence.

Of the four boys, Abdullah impressed Lawrence the most and, indeed, Abdullah would prove himself to be a strong ruler in the years ahead. "I began to suspect him of constant cheerfulness," Lawrence wrote. "His eyes had a confirmed twinkle; and though only thirty-five, he was putting on flesh. It might be due to too much laughter. Life seemed very merry for Abdulla[h]. He was short, strong, fair-skinned, with a carefully trimmed brown beard, masking his round smooth face and short lips. In manner he was open, or affected openness, and [he] was charming on acquaintance. He stood not on ceremony, but jested with all comers in most easy fashion; yet, when we fell into serious talk, the veil of humour seemed to fade away. He then chose his words, and argued shrewdly."

World War I erupted in 1914. As mentioned earlier, the Turks entered the war on the side of the Central Powers. The British, seeking an ally in the Middle East, approached Sharif Hussein and offered him independence for the Arab states following the war if he would fight the Turks. Hussein agreed, and the Great Arab Revolt commenced in June 1916.

Lawrence was dispatched as a military adviser to Sharif Hussein and his sons. "I vowed to make the Arab Revolt the engine of its own success as well as handmaid to [the British army's] Egyptian campaign, and vowed to lead it so madly in the final victory that expediency should counsel to the Powers a fair settlement of the Arabs' moral claims," Lawrence wrote.

The Arabs fought hard. Their biggest victories came in 1918 when Arab fighters under Hussein's son Faisal drove the Turks out of Damascus.

In 1917, the British issued the Balfour Declaration, guaranteeing a Jewish homeland in Palestine. The Arabs reacted bitterly to the declaration, believing the promise of the British to Sharif Hussein included Palestine as part of their realm. Actually, the British turned out to be far more duplicitous than even the Arabs suspected. Unknown to the Arabs, the British had signed the Sykes-Picot agreement with France, essentially dividing up between the two European powers the former Ottoman-held territories at the conclusion of the war. Britain took Iraq and Palestine as well as the west bank of the Jordan River; France took Lebanon. Syria was split between the two countries—France took the capital of Damascus and most of the northern territory while Britain kept the land along the east bank of the Jordan. That was territory that Britain felt it needed

Fort, Azraq, c. 1910

The desert of east Amman contains many interesting historical sites that attest to the historic importance of the region. In Roman times, this was the frontier. Several forts built to hold the line and guard trade routes still exist, such as the fort at Azraq.

The fort probably has changed a great deal since T. E. Lawrence ("Lawrence of Arabia") stayed there for several days in 1917. In *Seven Pillars of Wisdom*, Lawrence described how he slept in a room with a leaking roof because no mortar had been used in the construction. He dramatically recounted tales of ghostly dogs howling outside in the night. He wrote about the "blue fort on its rock above the rustling palms, with the fresh meadows and shining springs of water," and of the fort's "unfathomable silence." Today, a road runs by the fort and a village has grown up around it.

This photograph is of the entrance gate in the fort's south wall. Its massive door still swings on its hinges. Above the door is an inscription that records the fact that parts of the fort had been rebuilt in 1237. However, a great deal of the original Roman masonry still remains.

to serve as a buffer between Palestine and Syria. Evidently, the British didn't trust the French, and feared invasion of Palestine from northern Syria.

Clearly, the British had sold out the Arabs. The war

ended in 1918. The Ottoman Eempire had collapsed. Britain, France, and the Arabs and Jews all believed they had claims to the former Ottoman territories. In 1921, Winston Churchill arrived in Cairo to sort out the mess.

❖ ❖ ❖

Churchill was one of Great Britain's greatest statesmen. He was an eloquent and persuasive speaker and a master politician. In later years, he would be elected prime minister and lead his country through World War II. In 1921, he served his government as colonial secretary, charged with maintaining the British government's far-flung—albeit dwindling—territories away from British shores.

He arrived in the Middle East to find a decidedly hostile group of Arabs and their leaders. He was met by Lawrence, whom Churchill enlisted as an adviser. On a tour of the region, Churchill and Lawrence stopped in Gaza in Palestine where they witnessed a riot staged by anti-Jewish demonstrators.

"I say, Lawrence—are these people dangerous?" Churchill asked. "'They don't seem to be too pleased to see us. What are they shouting?'"

Lawrence interpreted the words for his colonial secretary: "'Down with the British and down with Jewish policy!'"

Meanwhile, since the end of World War I, the Hashemites had laid their claims to the various Arab states. An Arab Congress meeting in Damascus proclaimed Faisal king of Syria. Abdullah took the throne in Iraq while Ali ruled the Hejaz. Sharif Hussein arrived in the Arabian city of Jiddah and proclaimed himself king of Arabia. Only Abdullah's rule would endure, and it would not be in Iraq.

In 1920 France laid its claim to Syria, deposing Faisal. Sharif Hussein would soon be a victim of a coup staged by Abdul Aziz ibn Saud; henceforth, the country would be known as Saudi Arabia. The Saudis would eventually swallow up the Hejaz, ending Hashemite rule there as well.

As for Abdullah, at the Cairo conference Churchill made it clear to Abdullah that the British would have Iraq. He also made it clear that the British intended to abide by the Balfour Declaration:

> You have asked me in the first place to repudiate the Balfour Declaration and to veto immigration of Jews into Palestine. . . . It is not in my power to do so, nor, if it were in my power, would it be my wish. The British Government have passed their word, by the mouth of Mr. Balfour, that they will view with favour the establishment of a National Home for Jews in Palestine, and that inevitably involves the immigration of Jews into the country. This declaration of Mr. Balfour and of the British Government has been ratified by the Allied Powers who have been victorious in the Great War; and it was a declaration made while the war was still in progress, while victory and defeat hung in the balance. It must therefore be regarded as one of the facts definitely established by the triumphant conclusion of the Great War. . . .

To compensate Abdullah, Churchill offered him authority over the lands of southern Syria along the eastern bank of the Jordan River. Churchill called it "Transjordan," meaning "across Jordan." To sweeten the deal, Churchill promised a British subsidy and British army officers to arm and train the Transjordan army—which Churchill suggested Abdullah use to protect Palestine.

Transjordan was hardly the prize Sharif Hussein or his sons had in mind when they dreamed of a vast Hashemite empire stretching from Damascus to Baghdad to Mecca. Indeed, the land Churchill offered to Abdullah covered just 34,500 square miles—roughly the size of the state of

Dromedary, near Ma'an, 1912

The dromedary, or single-humped camel, can flourish on the coarsest of sparse vegetation. It feeds on the thorny plants and dried grasses that other animals would refuse. The dromedary is known to be able to go without water for 17 days and survive. When used for riding, as in this photograph, the animal can maintain a speed of 8–10 miles per hour for several hours.

Indiana. Amman, which would be the capital, was hardly the cosmopolitan center of trade that visitors found in Damascus or Baghdad. What's more, the land was rocky and untillable—to this day barely 5 percent of the country is farmed. And, finally, there were no known oil reserves in Transjordan. Some 80 years later, there are still none.

Churchill told Abdullah that he expected him to rule as a constitutional monarch, meaning the people of Transjordan would elect a parliament, although Abdullah, as emir, or prince, would have final authority over affairs of state. Churchill said a diplomat from Great Britain would be dispatched to Amman to advise the new government. Churchill also made it clear that Transjordan would, for the time being, remain under a British mandate—that it would exist as a state within the British Empire. There would be no immediate independence for the new nation, but Churchill promised Abdullah that could come in time.

Abdullah had no choice. On the morning of March 30, 1921, he accepted Churchill's offer.

The colonial secretary returned to England, where greater challenges would await him. By creating Transjordan, Churchill was certain that he fulfilled the pledge the British government made to Sharif Hussein in 1916.

But Lawrence knew the truth. He wrote:

> The Cabinet raised the Arabs to fight for us by definite promises of self-government afterwards. Arabs believe in persons, not in institutions. They saw in me a free agent of the British Government, and demanded from me an endorsement of its written promises. So I had to join the conspiracy, and, for what my word was worth, assured the men of their reward. In our two years' partnership under fire they grew accustomed to believing me and to think my Government, like myself, sincere. In this hope they performed some fine things, but, of course, instead of being proud of what we did together, I was continually and bitterly ashamed.

The Royal Tombs, Petra, c. 1920

It is thought that these large tombs held the remains of the Nabataean kings. The Nabataeans had a monopoly on trade caravans that passed from the Arabian interior to the coast. This was the chief source of their wealth. Strabo, the Greek geographer (first century A.D.), described Petra as a cosmopolitan city where foreigners mingled with the local inhabitants, who lived in luxurious villas. The city had a "democratic" monarch who dwelt in a "great house."

3
The War
of 1948

hen Abdullah arrived in Transjordan he found unforgiving deserts and rocky mountains. Amman, the capital of his country, was certainly no desert oasis, but it did have a railroad depot and was an important stop on a railway that connected Damascus with the city of Medina in the Hejaz.

Despite the hardscrabble nature of the country, there were indications that people had carved civilizations out of the Transjordan wilderness long before Churchill conceived the country during the Cairo summit.

In about 600 B.C. a nomadic tribe known as the Nabataeans arrived in the land now called Transjordan and established the city

Petra

The ancient city and mountain fortress of Petra, in southern Jordan, was the capital of the Nabataeans, peoples of ancient Arabia whom the Romans conquered in 106 A.D. In this remote desert stronghold, the Nabataeans created one of the most unusual cities of the ancient world.

We know that Petra was used as a crusader outpost in the 12th century. Then, for more than 600 years, it remained unknown to the Western world. In 1812, Jean Louis Burckhardt (1784–1817), a Swiss convert to Islam, "re-discovered" Petra enroute from Syria to Cairo. Burckhardt described his adventure in his still highly readable memoir, *Travels in Syria and the Holy Land* (1822).

Today, Petra is far and away Jordan's most spectacular tourist site.

Nabataean Tomb, c. 1920

Petra is best known for its dramatic tomb and temple facades, which its Nabataean Arab inhabitants carved into the soft sandstone some 2000 years ago.

Temple Facade, 1922

known as Petra, where the homes, temples, tombs, and other buildings were carved out of solid rock. Petra was located so deep in the mountains that it remained undiscovered until the late 19th century, when archaeologists stumbled on the ruins. The only way to enter the city was through a narrow, winding gorge. The Nabataeans were skilled engineers;

apparently, they conceived of a way to channel water into their mountain city.

The country is also the location of the Iraq el Amir—the "Caves of the Prince." The 11 caves are cut into the side of a mountain and are believed to have been hand-carved some 6,000 years ago.

Other sites of historical importance in Transjordan are Jerash, a city built by Greek conquerors in about 300 B.C., and Ajilun, site of a 12th-century Arab castle named Qala'at al-Rabad, which was built atop a 4,000-foot mountain. Indeed, it seemed to Abdullah that a people resourceful enough to carve a city out of stone or erect a castle atop a mountain were up to the task of building Transjordan.

But while there was no shortage of ancient ruins across the Transjordanian landscape, there was a definite lack of everything else. There were no hospitals and just a handful of schools. There were few paved roads, few farms, and no industry.

And there were few Transjordanians. None of the 300,000 people living in Transjordan in 1921 regarded themselves as Transjordanians; they were Syrians, Arabians, Iraqis, or Bedouins—the nomadic tribesmen who had crossed the Transjordanian frontier for centuries. For the most part, though, Transjordan was populated by Palestinian Arabs. About two-thirds of the new country's citizens considered their true home to be on the other side of the Jordan River—a fact that would be driven home to Abdullah and his successors for decades to come.

Abdullah found himself virtually the only leader in the Arab world willing to recognize the creation of a Jewish state on the western bank of the river and beyond. Abdullah realized a Jewish state would one day rise there and he aimed to live in peace with his neighbors. During the first decade of Transjordan's existence, Abdullah invited Jewish engineers into the country to help build roads and power plants. Other non-Muslims also became instrumental in developing the country. In 1936, Palestinian Christians discovered phosphate deposits in Transjordan. Today, the substance, which is an important ingredient of fertilizer, is the country's largest export.

Still, throughout its first decades of existence, Transjordan was a poor country. Abdullah and other members of the royal family shared in that poverty. A residence for the emir was not constructed until 1925; until that time, Abdullah lived modestly in the homes of tribal leaders, who were honored to share their quarters with the emir. For several months each year Abdullah lived as a Bedouin, pitching his tent in the desert near the Dead Sea after a long march atop a camel. At night, he would dine with friends in his tent. It was a lifestyle he preferred.

Other members of his family were not as fortunate. On November 14, 1935, his grandson Hussein ibn Talal was born. Hussein was the son of Talal, the crown prince, and his wife, Princess Zein. Talal and his family lived in a modest, unheated home in Amman. Hussein's baby sister would later die of pneumonia, and Talal was beginning to show signs of deteriorating mental health.

Meanwhile, the British kept their promise to arm and train a Transjordanian army. Major John Bagot Glubb was dispatched from the British military to create an army for Abdullah. Under Glubb, the Transjordanian army, known as the Arab Legion, would become the best-trained and hardest-fighting army in the Arab states.

In addition to Glubb, a number of British advisers served duty in Amman. Abdullah barely tolerated most of these advisers, finding them to be meddlers who failed to understand Arab ways and looked on Transjordan as a British colony under their authority. It seemed to Abdullah that the British government's representatives in his capital were interested more in looking after British interests

Major John Bagot Glubb, c. 1951

Major Glubb was a member of the British military who helped create an army for King Abdullah. This Transjordanian army, which was known as the Arab Legion, became the hardest-fighting army in the Arab states.

than in solving his country's enormous problems.

An exception was Alec Kirkbride, a former British army major assigned to the job in 1939. Kirkbride and Abdullah grew very close; Kirkbride would remain in Amman as an adviser to the emir and later as British ambassador to the country until Abdullah's death in 1951.

Across the river, establishment of a Jewish state had stalled. Although Jewish immigration to Palestine increased in the 1920s and 1930s, the British government failed to create a Jewish state acceptable to both Jews and Palestinian Arabs. The bitterness toward the British government by the Jews and Arabs often turned violent. In 1936, Palestinian Arabs rebelled against the British, who put down the revolt with considerable brutality. Jews were also making life difficult for the British. Jewish terrorist groups formed and targeted British officials.

While Jews and Arabs bickered over territory in Palestine, the British were forced to concentrate on more dire developments elsewhere in the world: In Germany, Adolf Hitler had come to power. This event had a profound impact on the future of Transjordan and the new Jewish settlement.

At the war's end, the German government was made to pay huge war reparations to France and other countries devastated by years of combat. Germany's financial obligations bankrupted the country; unemployment was high and inflation spiraled out of control. The government was threatened by bomb-throwing anarchists preaching a communist takeover, similar to the actions of the Bolsheviks in Russia. The German people were hungry, out of work, and desperate. Chaos reigned in their streets. They found themselves willing to accept the lies and grand promises made to them by charismatic leaders hungry for power. Hitler was one such leader. He promised to rebuild Germany and once again make the vanquished nation a world power. He told Germans they were the master race of Europe, far superior to the Poles or Russians, and, most of all, the Jews. In fact, Hitler blamed the Jews for the ills that had fallen on Germany.

Shortly after taking power in 1933, Hitler and his Nazi

followers started seizing Jewish property, forcing Jewish merchants out of business, and denying Jews certain rights and freedoms. On November 9, 1938, Nazi thugs took to the streets, smashing the windows of Jewish shops, setting synagogues on fire, and roughing up and arresting Jewish citizens. In Germany, it became known as Kristallnacht—Night of Broken Glass.

Soon, Jews were being herded into concentration camps where they were starved, made to perform slave labor, or murdered in gas chambers. By 1945, the year World War II ended, the Nazi regime would have to take responsibility for what has become known as the Holocaust—the killing of 6 million Jews.

To escape the Nazis, 300,000 Jews emigrated to Palestine during the war. They were joined after the war by concentration camp survivors. By 1947, some 600,000 Jews lived in Palestine.

The Jews demanded independence for their country and were dissatisfied with the British, who had failed to find an acceptable plan for Jewish statehood. Two terrorist groups, known as the Irgun and the Stern Gang, targeted Arab and British forces. On July 22, 1946, the Irgun blew up the King David Hotel in Jerusalem, site of the British army's headquarters. The gangs also sabotaged bridges, roads, and railroads and ambushed army barracks and airfields. In one sensational incident, two British army soldiers were kidnapped and murdered by the Irgun.

The British had had enough. Weary from six years of war with Germany, they were in no mood to give up their lives to defend Palestine. In April 1947 the British government asked the newly-formed United Nations (U.N.) to resolve the crisis and end the British Mandate.

Following World War II, there was tremendous international sympathy for the Holocaust survivors, and on November 29, 1947, the U.N. officially sanctioned the

Adolf Hitler, c. 1937

Hitler's destruction of the European Jews led 300,000 Jews to emigrate to Palestine during World War II. After the war these numbers swelled to over 600,000. As a consequence of this displacement and the international sympathy over the Holocaust, in 1947 the U.N. devised a plan to partition this territory into a new Jewish state of Israel and to set aside the West Bank lands for Arab settlement.

creation of a Jewish state in Palestine. Under the terms of the U.N. agreement, Palestine would be subjected to a complicated partitioning, in which most of its territory would become the new Jewish state, known as Israel, while a smaller territory, known as the West Bank, directly along the Jordan River, would be designated for Arab settlement.

The historic city of Jerusalem, site of important Jewish and Muslim shrines, would become an international zone under the authority of the U.N.

Jews were not entirely happy with the plan, particularly concerning the status of Jerusalem; nevertheless, they rejoiced. Arabs, however, seethed over the terms, believing them to be far more favorable to the Jews. Indeed, to the Arab citizens of Palestine, it seemed as though their desires were being ignored.

"The Palestinian Arabs had at present no will of their own," suggested Folke Bernadotte, a Swedish diplomat sent to the Middle East to help mediate a settlement. "Neither have they ever developed any specifically Palestinian nationalism. The demand for a separate Arab state in Palestine is consequently relatively weak. It would seem as though in existing circumstances most of the Palestinian Arabs would be quite content to be incorporated in Transjordan."

Following the war, the British finally relinquished their mandate over the Transjordan emirate. On March 26, 1946, Abdullah negotiated a treaty with the British that granted full independence to the country. On May 25, the parliament declared Abdullah king. The new name of the country would be the Hashemite Kingdom of Jordan.

It appeared Abdullah's first duty as king would be to lead his country into war. Violence broke out soon after the U.N. vote; riots erupted in Palestine, and 62 Jews and 32 Arabs were killed in the first seven days following the vote. Despite Abdullah's high regard for the Jews and his desire to live in peace with a Jewish state, the king found that he could not abandon the Arab citizens across the Jordan River. Further complicating matters was the status of Jerusalem, which was geographically located in the West Bank territory but which, under the U.N. vote, would remain an international city. Neither the Jews nor the Arabs were satisified with that "solution."

By the spring of 1948, there appeared to be no hope for a peaceful resolution. Both sides took up arms. One of the first major battles was fought at Deir Yassin, an Arab village that overlooked the highway leading to Jerusalem. Deir Yassin was considered strategically important because a well-armed group of soldiers hidden in the village could ambush convoys and troops heading for Jerusalem. About 100 members of the Irgun attacked the town on April 9. They were met with armed resistance by villagers. The siege took hours. Some 200 Arabs were killed in the fighting, while the Irgun lost four soldiers. Both sides claimed atrocities were committed during the fighting: Jews declared that Arabs who surrendered hid guns in their robes, then opened fire on their unsuspecting captors, while Arabs said the Irgun targeted civilians during the battle.

Jordan's Arab Legion struck back on May 4, 1948, attacking the Jewish settlement of Kfar Etzion. After a day of fierce fighting, the Arabs were forced to retreat. They returned a week later and laid siege to the settlement for two days, finally overrunning the badly outnumbered defenders. Many of the Jews were massacred after they surrendered. Kfar Etzion would turn out to be one of the few Jewish losses in the war.

Abdullah announced that he would send the Arab Legion across the Jordan River to Palestine to defend the Arabs living there. Other Arab nations supported Jordan. Egypt, Lebanon, Syria, and Iraq joined the coalition as well, forming, with Jordan, the Arab League.

"[A]ll our efforts to find a peaceful solution to the Palestine problem have failed," declared Abdullah. "The only way left for us is war. I will have the pleasure and honor to save Palestine."

Israel's Independence Day was set for May 14, 1948, the day the British Mandate officially ended. On May 15, the armies of five Arab nations attacked Israel.

On paper, it appeared the Jews were vastly outnumbered. After all, Israel's population was 600,000; the defenders would be facing armies representing a combined population of some 40 million Arabs. The Jews were also poorly armed—most of their weapons were smuggled into Israel from Czechoslovakia, paid for by Jewish benefactors in America and Europe. As for the army, it consisted of just 18,000 trained soldiers, although 10,000 refugees took up arms and fought alongside the army regulars. Even so, the army did not own a single tank or cannon. The air force consisted of eight obsolete Messerschmitt fighters, left over from World War II. The Israelis had found them in Czechoslovakia and had them disassembled and shipped to Israel, where they were reassembled virtually overnight. Looking over his ragtag army and its bargain-basement weapons, army chief Yigael Yadin told Prime Minister David Ben-Gurion: "The best we can tell you is that we have a 50/50 chance."

As it turned out, they were far better off than most of their Arab counterparts. The Arab League sent some 20,000 soldiers into Israel. The Egyptian, Syrian, Iraqi, and Lebanese armies were poorly trained, their leaders confused, their tactics questionable, and their men lacking the will to fight. The Jews, in contrast, were fearless combatants—they fought hard, determined this time not to be exterminated by an aggressive foe. They easily routed the Arabs in the early battles. Only Abdullah's Arab Legion held its own in the fighting, but it was hampered by the king's orders not to attack Jewish settlements. Abdullah insisted that the Arab Legion's job was to defend Palestinian Arabs, so he limited the Legion's role to defensive strategies.

An example of the Arabs' hapless military effort could be found near the Israeli village of Ashdod, south of the city of Tel Aviv. On May 29, a column of some 500 Egyptian armored vehicles and cannons was spotted approaching the village; clearly, the column's intentions were to surround Tel Aviv and lay siege to the city. The Israelis responded by scrambling their air force, with four of the aging Messerschmitts dispatched to attack the column.

The Israeli planes found the column stalled at a bombed-out bridge just 20 miles from Tel Aviv. Suddenly, they swooped down at the startled Egyptians, spraying the column with gunfire. The Egyptian soldiers panicked, abandoned their trucks and made for cover, never realizing that the machine guns firing at them were malfunctioning and few shots were hitting their marks.

While the Egyptian soldiers were waiting out the air raid, Israeli ground troops caught up with and ambushed the column and halting the advance and saving Tel Aviv. It was a stunning victory for the Israelis.

The bombed-out bridge was renamed "Gesher Ad Halom," a Hebrew phrase that means "Until Here." Only one of the Israeli pilots had died in the mission when his Messerschmitt had crashed and burned. The pilot, a South African–born Jew named Eddie Cohen, would be regarded as a national hero in Israel.

Abdullah's Arab Legion fared much better. Four days after the start of the war, the Jordanian troops under the leadership of John Bagot Glubb made their way to the outskirts of the Old City, the walled enclave of holy shrines within Jerusalem. Other Jordanian troops reached Latrun just west of Jerusalem, which enabled them to control routes to Jerusalem from the Israeli cities of Tel Aviv and Haifa. From its positions, the Arab Legion was able to hold off advancing Jewish soldiers. By early June, when a United Nations–brokered peace was declared, the battle for Jerusalem stood at a stalemate with the Jordanians in control of the Old City.

A truce was negotiated by Folke Bernadotte and took

effect on June 11. To end the war, Bernadotte offered to redraw the lines of the U.N. partition. However, under this Bernadotte plan, the status of Jerusalem would remain unclear. Neither side accepted the plan, and hostilities resumed on July 10.

Jordan's Arab Legion suffered the brunt of the new Israeli advance. Within two days of the resumption of fighting, Arab Legion troops were routed from a dozen key villages between Jerusalem and Tel Aviv, as well as from Lod Airport, the largest airport in the Middle East. Other Arab soldiers were sent on the run as well.

A second truce was declared July 18, although neither side adhered to its terms and sporadic fighting continued for nearly another year. Abdullah pushed the other Arab leaders for a permanent cease-fire, but his pleas were regarded with skepticism by his fellow rulers, who believed his real aim was to absorb Palestine into Jordan. In fact, just before the first truce, when the Arab Legion controlled Jerusalem, Abdullah met in Cairo with Muslim leader Hajj Amin, who made it clear to Abdullah that he did not favor Jordan's expansion plans. And, while the second truce was in effect, Arab leaders—without Abdullah's participation—created the "Government of All Palestine," with its seat in the Egyptian-controlled territory of Gaza along the Mediterranean Sea. Indeed, even as the Egyptians were still at war with the Israelis, they armed Palestinian Arabs and organized attacks on Jordanian troops.

The Government of All Palestine was short-lived. The Israelis, seemingly unstoppable, arrived in Gaza in October and ejected the Egyptians.

By March 1949 four of the five Arab nations had agreed to sign a treaty with Israel. Only Iraq refused to sign, but, certainly, the Iraqis were in no position to carry on the war themselves. Iraqi troops returned to Baghdad, and the

Israeli War of Independence was over. Jordan formally signed the treaty with Israel on April 3.

The war was a devastating loss to the Arabs. They wound up with less territory than what was guaranteed them under the United Nations partition plan of 1948.

Under the terms of the April 3 treaty, Jordan retained control of the West Bank, where some 500,000 Palestinian refugees were now living in squalid and overcrowded refugee camps. Another 100,000 refugees crossed the river, finding haven in Jordan itself. Many of those refugees looked for a scapegoat—someone to blame for the Arabs' defeat in the war and the loss of their homeland to the Jews.

It didn't take them long to find the scapegoat they sought in King Abdullah.

Arab Refugees, c. 1948

Arab refugees streamed out of what was then Palestine on the road to Lebanon in northern Israel to flee the fighting in the Galilee region during the Arab–Israeli War of 1948.

4

The
Little King

amal al-Gashey was born in a Palestinian refugee camp. In 1948, his family had fled from the Galilee region of Israel, and for the next several years they moved from one refugee camp to another. In the camps, refugees lived in tents or huts they built out of scraps of wood and tin. Disease was rampant, water often scarce. The children wore rags, and their shoes were often made from old rubber tires. Meager rations of food were provided by the United Nations Relief and Works Agency; families often went hungry.

"I was raised on my family's stories about Palestine, the paradise we were driven from, about how the Jews had stolen our land and expelled us from it, how the Arab leaders had betrayed us," al-Gashey said. "When I was growing up, I thought that there was no future for us unless we returned to Palestine, and that if we didn't return, I would spend my whole life as a refugee, deprived of any kind of human rights."

In 1950, King Abdullah annexed the West Bank. The Jordanian Parliament also passed laws extending citizenship to all Palestinian refugees. For Abdullah, these were bold and dangerous moves. By annexing the West Bank, Abdullah took the exact action the other Arab leaders had feared during the 1948 war—that he would take advantage of the war to extend his country's borders. By making Palestinians citizens of Jordan, he increased the population of his country by a third. What's more, native Jordanians were now a minority in Jordan. Before the war, the population had been evenly split, with about 500,000 Palestinians and 500,000 Jordanians. Now, with the addition of another 600,000 refugees, the Palestinians outnumbered the native Jordanians more than two to one.

The other Arab nations refused to recognize the West Bank annexation as well as the Jordanian citizenship of the Palestinians. Arab leaders were still determined to drive the Israelis out of Palestine and reclaim the land for the Palestinians. Making the refugees Jordanians, Arab leaders feared, they would cause them to relinquish their claims to Palestine.

In the camps, the refugees seethed at their circumstances and quickly focused on Abdullah as the culprit. They were convinced he had sold them out, purposely losing the war so that the West Bank would become his to annex. By 1951, the plots against his life were numerous. Abdullah's security forces were able to sniff out most of them, but on July 20 he ignored their warnings and walked into the ambush at the mosque in Jerusalem.

The reign of his 40-year-old son Talal was short. For years, Talal had suffered from schizophrenia, and within months the illness became apparent to government leaders in Amman. The Jordanian parliament was forced to remove Talal from power.

Parliament turned to Talal's son Hussein, who was named crown prince just months before Talal's removal. During his father's brief reign, Hussein had been sent to school in England. When he returned to Amman he was just 16 years old. Under Jordanian law, Hussein could not take the throne until he turned 18, so for the next two years the government of Jordan was administered by the cabinet, which was composed of men appointed by Abdullah. They were well aware that Hussein had been the old king's favorite and his choice to eventually succeed him. They were thus fiercely loyal to Hussein and protected his life closely. On May 2, 1953, Hussein became king of Jordan.

To diplomats, he was known as "the Little King," a nickname due mostly to his diminutive stature—Hussein stood just five feet four inches tall. But also, the nickname reflected what appeared to be his unwillingness to take his rule seriously; Hussein soon earned a reputation as a playboy who loved parties and the company of beautiful women. Many observers believed Hussein had no interest in the government and would leave the chores of running the country to others.

Meanwhile, in the rest of the Arab world, power was changing hands as well—usually with a large dose of violence. In Syria, two violent coups were staged by army officers in 1949. In Iraq, army officers murdered members of the royal family. In Egypt, the 1949 treaty with Israel touched off three years of rioting and assassinations that ended in 1952 with the exile of King Farouk. Army officers took command and, eventually, a colonel named Gamal Abdel Nasser seized control of the government. Nasser would prove to be a devious and influential player in Middle East affairs for the next 20 years.

King Saud of Saudi Arabia with President Nasser of Egypt (right), c. 1964

Gamal Abdel Nasser came to power in Egypt in 1952 and was an influential force in Middle East affairs for the next 20 years. Nasser was the Arab world's most vehement enemy of Israel.

And so King Hussein took power during a time of great turbulence—in Jordan as well as in other nations in the Middle East. The boy king would waste little time placing his signature on the growing tensions.

To rule Jordan, Hussein knew he would need the

unquestioned loyalty of the Arab Legion. Although the Legion had fought bravely in 1948, there had been a considerable amount of grumbling in the ranks among Jordanian soldiers since the end of the war about their British leaders. They had been led since the 1920s by the British army officer John Bagot Glubb, and other English soldiers held high ranks in the Arab Legion as well.

Glubb and the other English officers were singled out by Nasser as well as Palestinian leaders as proof that Hussein was under the influence of foreigners. Arab radio broadcasts as well as Arab newspapers aired daily attacks on Glubb.

Hussein decided he had no choice but to dismiss Glubb. The young king knew that by sacking Glubb he would risk the wrath of the British government, which was still providing the Arab Legion with $25 million a year in aid. But on March 1, 1956, Glubb was summoned to the office of Prime Minister Samir Rifai, who told him: "His Majesty the King orders that you take a rest."

"Is he annoyed about something?" Glubb responded. "I had a long and very cordial audience with him only yesterday. What is wrong?"

The prime minister declined to answer, asking simply, "Can you leave immediately?"

Glubb asked him what he meant by "immediately."

"Say at 4 o'clock this afternoon," Rifai responded. "We will give you an airplane."

Glubb and his family were hurried to a waiting plane, where they were whisked out of Jordan—quite an ignominious send-off for the man who had built the Arab Legion into the Middle East's best fighting force; nevertheless, Hussein aimed to show his soldiers that the Jordanian army would be under the command of Jordanian officers. As for the British, they soon ended Jordan's military subsidy.

While Hussein scored an important victory among his people by firing Glubb, his next move was a mistake. He elevated Colonel Ali abu Nawar to head the Arab Legion. Later, Nawar would lead an ill-fated coup against the king.

Across the Jordan River, the Israelis were busy building their country. Shortly after the end of the war, the Israelis had elected a parliament, known as the Knesset; one of the first acts of the Knesset was to pass the "Law of Return," granting Israeli citizenship to any Jew willing to emigrate to Israel. By 1951, some 700,000 Jews had emigrated to Israel, doubling the size of the young nation's population. Many were from European nations, but many were also from the Arab states—virtually the entire Jewish populations of Libya, Yemen, and Iraq left their homes for Israel.

The Arab states aimed to isolate Israel, so they resolved not to trade with the Jews, or with any western nation that carried on trade with Israel. Tensions reached a boiling point by the summer of 1956, when Egypt's Nasser nationalized the Suez Canal. Vital to Middle East shipping, the canal connects the Red Sea and the Nile River. It was built by French engineers in 1869 and had been owned since then by French and English shareholders under an agreement to turn it over to the Egyptian government in 1968. Security was provided in the Canal Zone by British troops.

But Nasser kicked out the French and British, took over the canal, and closed the waterway to ships bound for Israel. The United Nations Security Council ordered Nasser to open the canal, but the Egyptian president refused.

Both France and Great Britain had lost influence in the Middle East since the end of World War II; Nasser's seizure of the Suez Canal was the final outrage. Israel, France, and Great Britain hatched a plan to attack Egypt.

Meanwhile, leaders of the former Soviet Union saw the Middle East as a place where they could extend their influence and were happy to make arms available to Egypt.

On October 29, 1956, Israel sent troops across the Sinai desert into Egypt. By now, the Israeli army was 100,000

Hajj Fort, Ma'an, 1912

This centuries-old hajj fort was constructed to protect pilgrims en route to the holy city of Mecca in Arabia.

This photograph was taken in 1912 by Dr. Frank G. Clemow, the physician at the British Embassy in Constantinople. The Turkish government asked Dr. Clemow to select "the best site [along the Hejaz Railroad] for a pilgrims' quarantine station."

Clemow related his experiences in what is now southern Jordan at a meeting of the Royal Geographical Society in 1913. He described Ma'an as consisting of two villages—the closest to the railroad station was nearly a mile from it. The villages were mud-built, "well supplied with water and rich in gardens. A copious spring, yielding about 25 tons of water daily . . . exists about 500 yards from the station."

Today, Ma'an (pop. 35,000, 2000 est.) is a regional trade center for this sparsely settled southern part of Jordan.

soldiers strong, and it easily advanced over the sandy Egyptian plain. The United Nations Security Council proposed a resolution calling for the withdrawal of Israeli troops, but France and Great Britain blocked the motion. By November 5, with Israeli troops in control of the Sinai Peninsula, British and French paratroopers landed in the Canal Zone to seize control of the canal. In a separate attack, Israel took the coastal Gaza Strip, which adjoins the Sinai Peninsula.

Once again, an Arab army had been humiliated by Israel. What's more, the Sinai campaign had cost Egypt territory. At that point, the United States intervened. President Dwight D. Eisenhower brokered a peace that guaranteed Israeli troop withdrawal in exchange for Israel's right to use the Suez Canal for trade. Eisenhower was also alarmed at the Soviet influence in Egypt and regarded Nasser as an unstable dictator. And so he thus enacted the "Eisenhower Doctrine," which guaranteed American aid and military assistance to any Middle Eastern country threatened with communist aggression.

In Jordan, King Hussein expressed interest in the American offer, contrary to the wishes of many radical members of the Jordanian parliament, who wanted to see the country allied with the Soviets. They approached Ali abu Nuwar, who was then head of the Jordanian military, and convinced him to lead a coup attempt—one which ultimately failed when the king drew abu Nuwar to the town of Zerqa, where Hussein proved to the conspirators that he commanded the loyalty of the Jordanian soldiers.

There was no question, though, that by 1957 Jordan was desperate for money. The British had cut their aid the year before, following the firing of John Bagot Glubb. Saddled with responsibility for the Palestinian refugees and with no oil to sell and little farming and industry to generate revenue, the government of Amman had to turn to others for aid. After Hussein's overture to the Americans, the other Arab nations stepped in and offered to make up the subsidy. Saudi Arabia was quick to send money. Syria and Egypt also promised aid, but stalled on the payments and, instead, started disseminating anti-Hussein propaganda via the Arab print and broadcast media. In June, Jordan ended diplomatic relations with the two nations.

On Feburary 1, 1958, Egypt and Syria formed the United Arab Republic (U.A.R.). Nasser saw himself as the unquestioned leader of the Arab world, and it was clear to other Arab leaders that he intended soon to draw Jordan and Iraq into the alliance. The two countries formed an alliance of their own instead, but in July a military coup in Iraq deposed the royal family, ending the Iraq–Jordan pact.

King Hussein—now just 23 years old—found himself standing alone against the U.A.R. threat.

That summer, U.S. Navy vessels stationed in the Mediterranean Sea steamed to the region in a show of support for Hussein. The British, still fearing Nasser, forgave Hussein for sacking Glubb and sent troops, who took positions on Jordanian soil. Jordan was now a nation under protection by the wWestern powers, who were also allies of Israel. Nasser and other Arab leaders seethed at Hussein's involvement with the West, and vowed to oust the young king.

Following the failure of abu Nuwar's coup attempt, others made efforts to topple the king as well. On August 29, 1960, Hussein was hurrying to a meeting with Hazza al-Majali, his newly appointed prime minister, when two bombs planted in al-Majali's office exploded, killing the prime minister.

By the early 1960s, with American and British assistance, Jordan started slowly to climb out of the poverty that had plagued the nation since its founding. Jordanians developed cement and phosphate industries, and had in their country. What's more, Jordanians built a modern oil refinery in their country as well.

Hussein also found himself overseeing a construction boom: new homes and hotels were rising quickly out of the Jordanian desert, while the country's cities were being connected by highways that were among the most modern in the Middle East. Tourists were visiting Jordan as well;

the country still controlled the Old City in Jerusalem, site of some of the world's oldest religious landmarks.

As for his relations with Nasser and the other hostile Arab leaders, Hussein found them too caught up in their own squabbles to worry much about his country. In Yemen, Nasser had backed the losing side in a revolution, suffering still another humiliation. When Arab leaders met in 1964 in Cairo, Hussein and the other heads of state found Nasser to be far more humble and conciliatory toward them than he had been in the past. Apparently, Nasser had realized that he would never head a vast Arab empire, and that he would now have to forge alliances with his neighbors.

And so King Hussein surveyed all that he had accomplished and declared: "As Jordanians, we have learned one lesson that contributes daily to our progress: we have clarity of purpose. Having escaped death as a nation . . . Jordan wishes to play only one role, that of a model state. . . . We propose to devote . . . our full time and energy to the creation of a way of life that we hope in time all Arabs will achieve."

As it turned out, the king had painted too rosy a picture of life in Jordan. Since the end of the 1948 war, the Palestinians had remained in the West Bank refugee camps, and their cause seemed as hopeless as ever. For years, the refugees had allowed Hussein, Nasser, and the other Arab leaders to argue their cause. Now, it appeared they were ready to take matters into their own hands. They found ways to arm themselves and began plotting terrorist strikes on Israel.

At the 1964 Cairo conference, the Arab leaders embraced the idea of a Palestinian uprising and recognized the establishment of the Palestine Liberation Organization (PLO). Hussein agreed to support the PLO, but worried that the group would launch a war against Israel, who would then retaliate against the Arab states. Nobody needed to remind Hussein that Israel had fought two wars against the Arab nations and won both of them.

Shawbak (Shobak) Castle, 1920

Shawbak (Shobak) Castle is about 15 miles north of Petra. It was the first crusader castle built outside of the Kingdom of Jerusalem in what was then called the *Oultrejourdain*. The castle was constructed in 1118. The measurements of the doorway, and of the building, can be estimated from the height of the man standing to the right of the arch.

The First Crusade began in 1095. The crusaders captured Jerusalem in 1099 after an appalling massacre of its inhabitants. In 1118, the Christian king of Jerusalem, Baldwin II (1118–31), led an expedition across the Jordan River as part of an expansionist policy. He founded this castle at Shawbak (Shobak). At this time, the lordship of Oultrejourdain was established with a chain of castles running southward from the Dead Sea. Although Jordan was never at the heart of the crusader kingdom, it was strategically important in guarding the eastern flank in the Christian kingdom from attack.

It was also known throughout the Arab world that the PLO included a radical element; various militant groups, including the Popular Front for the Liberation of Palestine and *Fatah*, from an Arabic word that means "conquest," were operating under the PLO umbrella. So Hussein sought controls over the PLO leaders, and was promised that the organization would take no military action without the consent of the Arab states.

Alas, while Hussein may have believed he had placed effective controls over the PLO, he had no way of controlling Syria and Egypt. The two countries smuggled arms into the Palestinian camps and urged the refugees to make terrorist strikes against Israelis on the other side of the border. In 1965, 35 raids were conducted against Israel. In 1966, Israeli citizens suffered 41 terrorist attacks. During the first four months of 1967, Palestinians launched 37 attacks on Israeli soil.

Hussein saw war with Israel brewing and was anxious to avoid a confrontation. He closed PLO headquarters in Jerusalem and had several PLO leaders arrested. But the Egyptians and Syrians continually agitated the radical elements of the PLO, urging them to attack. On May 15, 1967—Independence Day in Israel—Egyptian troops mobilized in the Sinai desert near the Israeli border. Three days later, the Syrian army arrived at the Golan Heights just north of Israel. On May 30, Hussein signed a defense pact with Syria and Egypt, mobilizing the Jordanian army along the Jordan River.

"Our forces are now entirely ready not only to repulse the aggression, but to initiate the act of liberation itself," said Syrian Defense Minister Hafez Assad. "The Syrian army, with its finger on the trigger, is united. . . . I, as a military man, believe that the time has come to enter into a battle of annihilation."

Israel did not wait to see what would happen next. At 7:14 A.M. on June 5, the Israeli air force scrambled and headed for Egypt, where it found all the Egyptian war planes parked on airport tarmacs while their pilots ate breakfast. Within two hours, more than 300 planes—the entire Egyptian air force—had been destroyed. The Israelis also caught the Syrians, Jordanians, and Iraqis asleep, and most of those countries' military aircraft were destroyed as well.

On the second day, Israeli tanks raced across the Sinai desert, met the Egyptian tanks head-on and soon rolled over them. The Jordanian army attempted an offensive into the West Bank, but was driven back across the Jordan River. In the Golan Heights, Syrian troops held their ground until June 9, but Israeli air strikes eventually routed them. By June 11, it was all over. Some 15,000 Egyptians, 2,500 Syrians, and 800 Jordanians died in combat.

The entire war had taken just six days. The Arabs suffered another humiliating defeat. Now, the Israelis were in control of the Golan Heights, the Gaza Strip, the Sinai desert, the West Bank, and the entire city of Jerusalem. Some 400,000 Palestinians living in the West Bank refugee camps fled across the river to Jordan.

Hussein remembered what had happened to his grandfather when he had lost a war to Israel. The king resolved that he would not suffer the same fate.

The City of Jerusalem

As a result of the Six-Day War in 1967 Jordan lost control of the eastern part of Jerusalem, which was known as the Old City.

5

Black September

n the weeks following the Six-Day War, King Hussein became convinced that eviction of the Jews from Israel was not a viable plan. Three times, the armies of the Arab nations had gone up against the Israel Defense Force and three times the Arabs had suffered humiliating defeats. Two decades before, Hussein's grandfather had been willing to recognize the right of Israel to exist. Now, Hussein was ready to make the same concession. Immediately, he called for a conference of Arab leaders so that he could convince them to adopt a similar policy.

"We either come out better off now as the result of genuine efforts of all of us to face up to things, or we face some extremely serious possibilities of deterioration in the Arab world," Hussein said. "Even our identity, our ability to maintain ourselves as nations, is involved."

Secretly, Hussein started meeting with Israeli officials.

Jordan lost the most in the war. The West Bank was the location of most of the country's farms; now they were in Israeli hands. What's more, the country was ill-prepared to deal with the new wave of refugees who fled the West Bank and were now forced to live in makeshift camps on the eastern shore of the Jordan River. Once again, Palestinians found the poverty and squalor of the camps unbearable. Hussein encouraged the Palestinians to leave the camps and find jobs in the Jordanian economy, but most refused, believing that doing so would sacrifice their claims to their homeland.

Finally, Jordan lost control over eastern Jerusalem, location of the Old City. In 1948 the United Nations partition plan called for Jerusalem to remain under international jurisdiction and for its sacred shrines to be made accessible to all people. During the 1948 war, the Israelis captured the western half of the city, which contains the residential and business districts, while Abdullah's Arab Legion was able to hold on to and defend Jerusalem's eastern half, which includes the walled Old City. The Israelis moved the Knesset to their half of Jerusalem, declaring the city the capital of Israel. In 1950, Abdullah annexed the Old City as well as the remainder of the West Bank territory, making them part of Jordan.

But now, Jerusalem was entirely in the hands of the Israelis. Hussein as well as other Arab leaders vowed to win back the Old City and its sacred Muslim shrines.

But Jews and Christians regard Jerusalem as a holy city as well. In biblical times Jerusalem served as the home of King David and King Solomon, who built many palaces and other ornate buildings in the Old City. Solomon built a great house of worship, known as the Temple of Solomon, and also surrounded the city with a wall. Later, King Herod erected a great temple, the Western Wall of which remains standing today. Jews throughout the world make pilgrimages to the Western Wall, which they regard as one of their religion's most sacred sites.

According to Christians, Jesus Christ spent his last days on earth in Jerusalem. Also, during the era of the Roman Empire, the Church of the Holy Sepulcher was built by Emperor Constantine. Other rulers of Rome also erected Christian churches and, indeed, for centuries after the death of Christ the city was dominated by Christians.

But in the 7th century, Muslims swept into the city, drove out the Christians, and established their own shrines. It was during this period that the Dome of the Rock was built in Jerusalem. The mosque is built on the site where Muhammad is said to have ascended to heaven.

But the Dome of the Rock symbolizes more than just the birthplace of Islam. It is also a symbol of the conflict that exists between Jews and Muslims, because the Dome of the Rock is built over the altar of the Temple of Solomon. Following the Six-Day War, the Dome of the Rock was under the control of the Israelis.

Meanwhile, Hussein found his pleas for peace with the Israelis falling on deaf ears. Egyptian soldiers continued skirmishing with the Israelis just three weeks after the end of the war. The Soviet Union, anxious to maintain its influence in the Middle East, quickly resupplied Nasser's troops with the tanks, anti-aircraft guns, and aircraft lost in the Six-Day War. For three years, Egypt and Israel launched raids against each other's positions. Finally, in August 1970, Henry Kissinger, at the time the national security adviser to U.S. President Richard Nixon, brokered a peace between the two sides.

The Syrians were also loath to accept the outcome of the Six-Day War. Instead of launching direct attacks on

Israel, however, Syrian agents recruited and armed Palestinian terrorists living in Jordan's refugee camps. Soon, a leader of the Palestinians would emerge: Yasir Arafat, a short, plump, unshaven militant who had given up a career as a civil engineer for the Palestinian cause. Born in Egypt to Palestinian parents, Arafat attended Cairo University, where he led demonstrations calling for a Palestinian homeland. Following graduation, he found a job in a cement factory. In 1956, he was called to active duty in the Egyptian Army for the Sinai War, but found himself disagreeing with Nasser's call for a single Arab empire. Palestinians wanted self-rule; they didn't want to win back their homelands so they could be ruled by another Arab people. After the war, Arafat found work as an engineer in Kuwait, where he helped found Fatah—a militant organization devoted to armed uprisings.

At first, Arafat had nothing to do with the Palestine Liberation Organization. The group was founded in 1964 and its first chairman, Ahmed Shukairy, was mostly regarded as an uncouth windbag, barely tolerated by the Arab heads of state. Arafat and the other Fatah leaders had no interest in Shukairy's long-winded speeches. In 1965, Fatah boldly announced: "Let the imperialists and Zionists know that the people of Palestine are still in the field of battle and shall never be swept away."

At the time, Arafat was the leader of just 26 poorly armed fighters.

Help would soon arrive. Wealthy Saudi sheiks provided money for weapons, while in the refugee camps, Fatah found recruits. These *fedayeen* were armed and sent into Israel on terrorist missions.

In 1968 a Fatah bomb exploded under an Israeli school bus, killing an adult and one child and injuring 29 children. The response by the Israel Defense Force was swift. Israeli

Ahmed Shukairy, c. 1965

Shukairy was the first chairman of the PLO (Palestine Liberation Organization).
This group became increasingly important under the leadership of Yasir Arafat,
who later became chairman of the PLO.

agents traced the terrorists responsible for the bombing to
the village of Karameh in Jordan. On March 21, Israeli
commandos flooded into Karameh; they were met by Fatah
guerrillas who fought hard and managed to hold the
village. Israeli tank crews soon arrived, but Jordanian army
units arrived as well and—against Hussein's orders—
engaged the tank crews in battle. By the end of the day,
Karameh was leveled, but the Israelis had encountered
surprisingly strong resistance and suffered heavy losses.
Arafat, who claimed to have taken part in the fighting,
declared Karameh a Palestinian victory.

Karameh showed that Fatah could be an effective fighting force. By the end of 1968, some 2,000 recruits from the
refugee camps were members of Arafat's Palestinian army.
On February 3, 1969, the Palestine Liberation Organization

named Arafat its chairman, and Jordan became the base of his operations. From Jordan the PLO planned and launched its terrorist strikes at Israel.

By 1968, many of those attacks were aimed at planes flown by El Al, Israel's national airline. On July 23, 1968, an El Al plane en route to Israel from Rome was hijacked by Palestinian terrorists. After a forced landing in Algiers, the 42 passengers and crew members were held for five weeks, but finally released. On February 18, 1969, terrorists attempted to hijack an El Al plane at the airport in Zurich, Switzerland; a crew member and terrorist were killed in the exchange of gunfire. On February 10, 1970, an Israeli passenger was killed in an attempted hijacking of an El Al plane in Munich, West Germany.

Israel would strike back hard following such incidents, of which there were many. Hussein found his country constantly pounded by Israeli air strikes.

The PLO was causing Hussein other problems as well. More and more, Arafat seemed to be directing his harshest rhetoric at Hussein, whom he regarded as weak. In October 1968, thousands of fedayeen staged a demonstration and march through the streets of Amman, shouting anti-Hussein slogans. Clearly, Arafat aimed to demonstrate his power to the king.

What's more, the fedayeen were hardly proving to be welcome guests. Jordanians knew the Israeli air raids were launched in retaliation to Palestinian terror, and they wished the fedayeen to leave. What's more, many of the fedayeen committed petty crimes, roughing up and robbing Jordanians. Arafat promised Hussein he would rein in his troops, but before long it was clear to Hussein that things were out of control.

On June 7, 1970, American diplomat Morris Draper was kidnapped by terrorists in Amman. He was released after one day of captivity, but three days later another

American, U.S. Army Major Robert Perry, was murdered by terrorists.

On June 9, the fedayeen attempted to assassinate Hussein. Word had reached Hussein that fedayeen were attacking his intelligence headquarters. Accompanied by two aides and a squadron of soldiers, Hussein drove out to see for himself.

The motorcade was attacked at a crossroads. The king's Land Rover fell under heavy fire, forcing Hussein to jump out of the vehicle and into a roadside ditch. The two aides jumped after him and covered the king with their bodies. The Jordanian soldiers finally drove back the fedayeen assault, allowing Hussein to return to Amman.

"No one—adult or child—could be sure on leaving his house whether his family would see him again. Amman became a virtual battlefield," Hussein said. "No Regular Army people could enter the city in uniform, as they would be fired on by the PLO. . . . The people in the armed forces began to lose confidence in me."

What to do next? Hussein's more hard-line advisers, including his uncle, army commander Sharif Nasser bin Jamil, and Wasfi al-Tall, a former prime minister, urged Hussein to crack down hard on the fedayeen. Others, including Bahjat Talhouni, the current prime minister, urged the king to negotiate with Arafat. Unsure that anything could be accomplished, Hussein reluctantly agreed to talks with the PLO leader.

Hussein and Arafat negotiated a cease-fire, but the fedayeen promptly ignored it. Soon after the pact was signed, 68 people were taken hostage in two Amman hotels. On September 6, Swiss and American airliners were hijacked by terrorists and made to land at a remote Jordanian airstrip. Hussein dispatched troops to the airstrip, where they saw to the release of the passengers. The incident sparked skirmishes elsewhere in Jordan between fedayeen and the Arab Legion.

On September 17, 1970, Syrian tanks crossed over into Jordan to support the fedayeen. Now, the powder keg that Hussein had been sitting atop threatened to explode into an international situation. Hussein asked President Nixon to launch air strikes against the Syrians from a U.S. Navy task force anchored in the Mediterranean; Nixon refused, but suggested the Israelis may be willing to intervene. Indeed, the Israelis were willing. They considered Hussein a moderate and had been meeting secretly with the king since the Six-Day War. Still, Hussein knew that if he asked the Israelis to defend Jordan, he would be risking the wrath of the other Arab leaders who regarded Israel as their enemy. But there was no question that the Syrians aimed to overthrow Hussein and install a Palestinian-led government in Amman.

By September 19, the fighting was fierce. In the north, battling the Syrian invaders, while in Amman fedayeen and Jordanian soldiers fought in the streets. On September 20, Israel mobilized its air and ground forces in preparation, should Hussein authorize the strikes.

Ultimately, Hussein never had to ask for Israel's help. On September 22, the tide suddenly turned in favor of the Jordanian army. Syrian tanks had moved to within 50 miles of Amman, but that's where the advance ended. Jordan hit the Syrians with artillery fire, tanks, and air strikes. The Syrians had foolishly dropped their air cover for the advancing tank force, and the Jordanian jets strafed the tank crews at will. By the end of the day, more than 60 Syrian tanks were reduced to smoldering hulks in the Jordanian desert. Some 600 Syrian soldiers were killed in the battle.

But the fighting in the streets of Amman was still fierce. Such Arab leaders as Nasser in Egypt and Sudan President

Arab Heads of State Meet in Cairo, c. 1970

This meeting was an attempt to put an end to the civil war in Jordan between Palestinians and the government of King Hussein. This conference, moderated by President Nasser of Egypt, was not very successful due to the volatile and complicated nature of their differences. From left to right: Libyan leader Muammar Qaddafi, PLO leader Yasir Arafat, President Nasser, and King Hussein of Jordan.

Gaafar al-Nimeiri pressed Arafat and Hussein to call a truce, but by now Hussein was in no mood to back down. His troops had defeated the Syrians and were now concentrating on the street fighting in Amman. The fedayeen held out until September 25, when Arafat broadcast a message to the fighters over a radio station in Damascus in which he said:

> Our great people, our brave revolutionaries, to avoid more innocent bloodshed, and so that the citizens may care for their wounded and get the necessities of life, I, in my capacity as supreme commander of the Palestine revolutionary forces, and in response to the appeal by the mission of Arab heads of state, agree to a cease-fire and ask my brothers to observe it provided the other side does the same.

On September 27, Hussein met Arafat in a peace

conference in Cairo moderated by Nasser. Little was accomplished. Back in Jordan, the fedayeen were still armed and still a formidable military presence. For the next several months, Hussein ruled over an uneasy peace while he quietly re-armed his troops. The Americans and British were now willing to supply Jordan with weapons.

On March 26, 1971, the fedayeen attacked a Jordanian police station in Irbid, Jordan's second-largest city. Hussein unleashed the army with orders to drive the fedayeen from Irbid. On April 6, he ordered the fedayeen out of Amman. By now, greatly outnumbered, the fedayeen left without offering resistance. Elsewhere, the fedayeen were more stubborn. On June 1, a Jordanian farmer was killed by terrorists near the city of Jerash. Hussein ordered Wasfi al-Tall, who had been reappointed prime minister, "to take bold and tough action against the guerrillas."

Al-Tall dispatched the army into the refugee camps with orders to rout the fedayeen. Some 4,000 Palestinians were killed by the soldiers while thousands more were driven out of Jordan into camps in Lebanon and Syria. By July 1971 the fedayeen threat to Hussein had been eliminated.

"We dug our own graves in Jordan," an Arafat supporter said later. "We were welcomed as heroes after Karameh and then driven out like thieves in the night three years later. It did not seem to occur to us that although we shared a common language, culture and religion with the Jordanians, they were in fact in some ways different from us. Some of them had been living in Jordan for centuries and resented our appropriation of their country—or so it must have seemed to them."

The events that led up to the expulsion of the PLO from Jordan became known to Palestinians as "Black September," to mark the month in 1970 when Hussein put down the uprising. When PLO members resettled in refugee camps in Syria, Lebanon, and other Arab countries, they seethed with hatred for Hussein as well as for their old enemy Israel. Militant leaders in the camps formed a terrorist group with the aim of moving the conflict onto the world stage. They called themselves "Black September" and resolved to strike back at their two enemies.

Black September struck first in November 1971, murdering Jordanian Prime Minister Wasfi al-Tall. Assassins gunned him down outside a hotel in Cairo, Egypt. Egyptian police quickly closed in and apprehended three terrorists responsible for the murder. As terrorist Monzer Khalifa was led away, he shouted: "We are members of Black September!"

Three weeks later, King Hussein's unfriendly regime was again targeted by Black September. Zaid el Rifai, Jordan's ambassador to Great Britain, was attacked in downtown London by a terrorist wielding a machine gun.

"I couldn't believe it," said William Parsons, a London electric utility worker who witnessed the attack. "He levelled it at hip height, pulled the trigger, and loosed off about 30 rounds. It was like a scene from a Chicago gangster film."

Miraculously, el Rifai survived the attack—a bullet had sliced through his right hand, but otherwise he was uninjured. Nevertheless, the violence directed toward the prime minister and the ambassador served Black September's purpose—to establish itself as a ruthless terrorist organization, capable of striking quickly against its enemies.

Following the assassination of al-Tall and the attempt on the life of el Rifai, leaders of Black September turned their attention to their other sworn enemy: Israel.

In May 1972, four Black September members—Ahmed Mousa Awad, Abdel Aziz el Atrash, Therese Halasseh, and Rima Tannous—boarded a Sabena Airlines flight in

Brussels, Belgium, that was bound for Tel Aviv. Carrying guns and hand grenades, the four terrorists announced that they planned to start murdering the 91 passengers and crew members unless more than 200 Palestinian prisoners were released from Israeli jails.

The plane landed in Tel Aviv. On the ground, Israeli negotiators kept the talks with the terrorists going for 20 hours, until a special unit of commandos could be summoned and prepared for a siege on the plane. Dressed as ground crew members, the commandos suddenly rushed the plane and killed Awad and el Atrash. The two female terrorists, Halasseh and Tannous, were captured. One passenger was killed in the melee aboard the airliner.

On August 15, 1972, Halasseh and Tannous were sentenced by an Israeli court to life in prison.

In the refugee camps in Syria and Lebanon, Black September leaders bristled over the failure of the Sabena hijacking. Until then, few people outside the Middle East were aware of the plight of the Palestinians. And so Black September leaders met in Rome, Italy, and hatched a plan to draw international attention to their struggle: They planned to kidnap the Israeli Olympic team at the forthcoming Summer Olympic Games in Munich, West Germany, and demand the release of 236 Palestinians held in Israeli prisons.

Eight Palestinian terrorists carried out the plot in the early morning hours of September 5, 1972. They were able to sneak into the Olympic village, break down the doors of the apartments where the Israelis were living, and seize nine hostages. German authorities spent the next 17 hours trying to negotiate the release of the hostages, but the incident finally ended in a shoot-out at Fürstenfeldbruck, a German military airport. All nine hostages and two other people were murdered by the terrorists during the melee. German police managed to kill five terrorists; three were captured.

A month later, those terrorists were freed when Black September members hijacked a German airliner and threatened to kill the 17 passengers and crew members until the three Olympic terrorists were released. Rather than risk more deaths, the German police conceded to their demands.

Jordan River, 1922

Since 1948, the meandering Jordan River has marked the frontier between Israel to the west and Jordan to the east. (The river, the lowest in the world, is about 200 miles in length stretching from its sources in Syria and Lebanon to the Dead Sea. Christians, Jews, and Muslims alike revere the Jordan, and it is in its waters that Jesus is believed to have been baptized by St. John the Baptist.)

6

A Durable Peace

In September 1970, while King Hussein carried out the defense of his country against Syrian invaders, another event occurred in the Arab world that would have a radical impact on the Middle East. In Egypt, Gamal Abdel Nasser had been in ill health for some time, suffering from heart disease and diabetes. On September 28, he died of a heart attack.

Nasser had been the Arab world's most vehement enemy of Israel. What's more, he remained the lone Arab leader who believed all the Arab states of the Middle East could unite under one flag. With Nasser gone, that idea quickly died.

Nasser's successor was Anwar Sadat, who would prove to be a much different type of leader. He relaxed restrictions on Egyptians, allowing them more personal freedoms. He permitted Egyptian companies to trade with the West. He encouraged tourists to visit the pyramids, the Great Sphinx, and other ancient Egyptian wonders.

And he would take a decidedly different approach toward Israel.

But not immediately. During the Six-Day War, Egypt had lost the Sinai desert as well as control of the Suez Canal to Israel. On October 6, 1973, Sadat launched a surprise attack on Israeli positions in the Sinai. The attack occurred on Yom Kippur, the holiest day on the Hebrew calendar. Israelis were caught off guard by the assault and, in the first few days of fighting, were forced to retreat.

Syrian troops participated in the "Yom Kippur War" as well, attacking Israel from the north. During the first two days of the war, some 600,000 Arab troops; 2,000 tanks; and 550 aircraft advanced on the Israeli-held positions.

Jordan did not attack. Sadat and Syrian leader Hafez Assad planned the siege on their own without taking the Jordanian king into their confidence. It is doubtful, however, Hussein would have participated even if he had known the attack was coming. Although Hussein sent a token brigade of tanks to serve alongside the Syrians, the king had long ago concluded that no matter how overwhelming the odds seemed to be, Israelis always outfought Arabs. He had no intention of sacrificing his main force of soldiers to Israeli defenders. The Israelis were thankful for the king's reluctance to participate in the war; by not having to defend their border against a Jordanian advance, the Israelis were able to send more troops to the Egyptian and Syrian fronts.

At first, the war did not go well for Israel. Using modern weaponry supplied by the Soviet Union, the Egyptians and Syrians outmaneuvered the Israelis and inflicted tremendous damage to their defenses. Nevertheless, Hussein's assessment of Israeli courage under fire proved to be correct. The tide

Anwar Sadat, c. 1980

In Egypt Nasser was succeeded by Sadat, whose approach to Israel turned out to be radically different from Nasser's. In 1979, Sadat signed the Camp David Accord, which recognized Israel's right to exist. His assassination on October 6, 1981 is believed to be a result of his breaking ranks with the other Arab states.

soon turned in favor of the Israelis, who were aided by a massive airlift of American arms.

On October 12, the largest tank battle since World War II erupted in the Sinai desert when 1,000 Israeli and Egyptian tanks clashed. For three days, the two sides bombarded each other from sand dune to sand dune. By late afternoon on October 14, the Egyptians were in retreat. Four days later, Israeli troops were within striking distance of Cairo.

Meanwhile, in the north, Israeli troops pushed the Syrian attackers back across the Golan Heights and chased them back to Damascus. On October 12, Israeli soldiers stopped just short of the Syrian capital. It is likely that the Israelis would have invaded the capitals of Syria and Egypt, but the Soviet Union intervened and said it would send troops to stop the Israeli advance. The United States placed its troops on alert as well, which forced the Soviets to back down. On October 22, the Arabs and Israelis accepted the terms of a United Nations peace resolution: all the territory the Egyptians had seized in the first few days of the war was returned to Israel.

The Jordanians would be punished by the other Arab leaders for their refusal to fight in the Yom Kippur War. In 1974, at a summit of Arab leaders in Rabat, Morocco, Jordan was stripped of its responsibility for the Palestinians. The Arab leaders designated the PLO as the sole legitimate representative of the Palestinian people, and ordered Hussein to turn over the West Bank to the Palestinians should the Israelis return it.

This decision would prove to be incredibly short-sighted. As a moderate voice in the Middle East, Hussein was in a far better position to negotiate for the Palestinians than the hard-charging Arafat, who at the time was advocating nothing less than the destruction of the Jewish state. The Israelis respected Hussein and owed him a debt for staying out of the Yom Kippur War. By stripping Hussein of his responsibility for the Palestinians, the other Arab leaders delayed any Middle East peace negotiations for years, if not decades.

Once the Palestinian threat was removed from Jordan, the country settled in for a period of incredible economic growth. Although oil was never detected beneath Jordanian soil, the Jordanian people were able to take advantage of the oil boom. Some 400,000 Jordanian citizens worked in the petroleum industry for the neighboring oil-rich states; their

Hotel Bombing in Beirut, Lebanon, c. 1976

During Lebanon's protracted civil war the city of Beirut became a war zone. This resident of the Mayflower Hotel was critically wounded when a rocket hit the hotel.

taxes were sent home to support the Jordanian economy.

Amman became a banking center during the 1970s and 1980s, thanks to the Palestinians who fled Jordan for Syria and who soon found themselves unwelcome guests in that country as well. By 1975, President Assad had forced them to leave Syria; many Palestinians settled in Lebanon, location of many of the Middle East's major banks, causing that country to plunge into a civil war. The city of Beirut became a battle zone. When executives of the banks searched for a stable country where they could re-establish their businesses, they settled on Jordan.

Jordan had always been one of the few nations in the Middle East to enjoy a form of democracy. Although the Hashemite sovereign had always been the ultimate authority in the country, a parliament had given people representation in their government as far back as the 1920s. Following the Six-Day War, though, Hussein found it necessary to close parliament, curtail many personal freedoms, and impose martial law due to the threat posed by a potential Israeli invasion and, later, by the Palestinian uprising. Indeed, the last time Jordanians had elected members to a parliament had been in 1967—and half of those seats were held by members representing the West Bank, which was now under Israeli occupation.

By 1978, however, Hussein started to ease martial law and return personal freedoms to the Jordanian people. He created "National Consultive Councils" to temporarily replace the parliament. The councils, which were composed of representatives selected by the king, governed the nation until 1984, when Hussein decreed that elections could be held for a new parliament. The West Bank elected members to the new parliament, but its members were prohibited by Israel from taking their seats in Amman.

Arafat and other PLO leaders continued to agitate for Palestinian independence. Indeed, the PLO blamed Hussein for the woes of the Palestinian people. Palestinians continued to demonstrate against Hussein in the West Bank and even on the streets of Amman. In 1988, police arrested 23 Palestinians in Jordan and charged them with planning an overthrow of Hussein's government.

Finally, the king decided to give the West Bank Palestinians the opportunity for self-determination. On July 30, 1988, Hussein announced that he was dissolving parliament, which put an end to West Bank representation in the Jordanian government. The next night, he appeared on national television and announced that he had formally renounced

Jordan's claims to the West Bank and East Jerusalem. Hussein said he was ready now to accept the 1974 Rabat decree, which recognized the PLO as the official representative of the Palestinian people. He told Jordanians:

> [T]here is a general Palestinian and Arab orientation which believes in the need to highlight the Palestinian identity in full in all efforts and activities related to the Palestine question and its developments . . . It has also become clear that there is a general conviction that maintaining the legal and administrative links with the West Bank, and the ensuing Jordanian interaction with our Palestinian brothers under occupation through Jordanian institutions in the occupied territories, contradicts this orientation. It is also viewed that these links hamper the Palestinian struggle to gain international support for the Palestinian cause of a people struggling against foreign occupation.

On November 8, 1989, Jordanians elected a new parliament. For the first time in the country's history, women were permitted to vote and hold office. In many Islamic states, women hold hardly any rights at all, much less the right to vote and be part of their government.

The 1970s and 1980s also represented an era of change in the king's personal life. In 1977, the king's wife, Queen Alia, died in a helicopter accident while returning to Amman after visiting a hospital in the southern Jordanian city of Tafila. Hussein was devastated at the loss. His third wife (his first two marriages had ended unhappily), Alia Toukan was the daughter of a Jordanian diplomat. The couple had married in 1972, shortly after the king's second divorce.

King Hussein and Queen Noor, c. 1978

In 1978, Texas-born American Lisa Halaby became the fourth wife of King Hussein.

She was the daughter of a Syrian-born business executive and his Swiss wife. Queen Noor became an immensely popular figure in Jordan and has remained a visible spokesperson for her country even after the death of her husband in 1999.

The king spent several months in a deep fit of depression. But during a ceremony to dedicate a new jetliner for the Royal Jordanian Airline, the king was introduced to a young American architect named Lisa Halaby. The tall, strikingly beautiful woman was from Texas; she was the daughter of the Syrian-born business executive Najeeb H. Halaby and his Swiss wife.

They married in 1978. Lisa Halaby converted to Islam and took the name Lisa Noor Al Hussein, which means "Light of Hussein." To the Jordanian people, she was known as Queen Noor, and she would become an immensely popular figure among her husband's subjects. Hussein

called her "a Jordanian who belongs to this country with every fiber of her being."

❖   ❖   ❖

The Yom Kippur War proved to be a watershed event in the Middle East not only because of its impact on the Arab states, but also because of the effect it had on Israelis. Although they won the war, the Israelis suffered great losses in men and armaments. The Arabs had also been able to launch a surprise attack. Israeli intelligence had broken down. No longer could they consider themselves invincible to Arab invasion. After the war, Prime Minister Golda Meir resigned. Eventually, Menachem Begin was elected prime minister. He was a one-time Irgun commando who had used terrorist tactics to help Israel win independence in the 1948 war.

By the 1970s, Begin was far less militant. In 1977, he made an overture of peace to Sadat: Through secret channels, he offered to return the Sinai desert to the Egyptians if Sadat would sign a treaty guaranteeing peace with Israel. Sadat received the offer warmly; indeed, he shocked the world when he announced to the Egyptian parliament that he wished to travel to West Jersualem to address the Knesset. Begin immediately made a formal invitation, and on November 19, 1977, Anwar Sadat became the first Arab head of state to address Israel's parliament.

"I have come to you so that together we should build a durable peace based on justice to avoid the shedding of one single drop of blood by both sides," Sadat told the Knesset members. "It is for this reason that I have proclaimed my readiness to go to the ends of the earth."

There were many roadblocks in the way before the treaty would be signed. One of the barriers to the treaty was the fate of the Palestinian people in the West Bank; Sadat insisted they be granted independence, but Begin was not ready to give up the territory. By now, Jews had established settlements in the West Bank. Begin suggested the Palestinians be given the right to govern themselves, albeit under the flag of Israel.

The two sides remained deadlocked for months. Finally, U.S. President Jimmy Carter stepped into the negotiations and invited Begin and Sadat to attend a summit meeting at Camp David, the presidential retreat in Maryland. On September 5, 1978, Begin, Sadat, and Carter arrived in the bucolic hills of Maryland for the history-making summit.

After 12 days of intense negotiations that often appeared on the verge of failure, Begin, Sadat, and Carter signed what became known as the Camp David Accords. Under the Accords, Egypt agreed to recognize Israel's right to exist. Israel, in turn, agreed to withdraw from the Sinai and provide autonomy to the Palestinians in the West Bank as well as Gaza within five years. On March 26, 1979, Begin and Sadat signed a treaty on the White House lawn.

The other Arab leaders were appalled. They seethed over the Camp David Accords, accusing Sadat of treason to the Arab cause. Certainly, it was true that Nasser and other Arab leaders had never been able to forge a unified Arab empire and that the Arab heads of state were prone to bickering, treachery, and ambition. Nevertheless, when it came to Israel, the Arab leaders had always spoken with a single voice, and that voice had always called for the destruction of the Jewish state. Now, Sadat had broken ranks and obtained a separate peace. Even King Hussein, believed to be a moderate, criticized Sadat for taking the peace initiative.

"The Egyptians are free to do whatever they think best, although, morally, I feel they should take into consideration the interests of the people who've suffered beside them in combat," admonished the king.

Anwar Sadat would pay with his life for making peace

with Israel. On October 6, 1981, five Egyptian army soldiers suddenly stepped out of the ranks of a military parade in Cairo and attacked the reviewing stand where Sadat and other leaders of the government were seated. The terrorists hurled grenades at the stand and sprayed the dignitaries with machine-gun fire. Twelve people were killed in the attack, including the president of Egypt. The terrorists were quickly captured and eventually executed. Later, the Egyptians learned the killers had been backed by Libyan dictator Muammar Qaddafi, who was one of the staunchest critics of the Camp David Accord in the Arab world.

Egypt survived the assassination of Sadat. The new president, Hosni Mubarak, remained as committed to the Camp David Accord as his predecessor. Meanwhile, Egypt maintained peace at home.

Other Middle East nations were far less fortunate. In Iran in the 1970s, the long-time ruler, Shah Mohammad Reza Pahlavi, was overthrown during a fundamental Islamic revolution led by exiled religious leader Ayatollah Ruhollah Khomeini. The shah had been friendly to the United States, but when he was ousted, Khomeini declared America the enemy of Iran. In 1979, Islamic militants stormed the U.S. Embassy in Tehran and took 52 embassy workers hostage. They were held by the Iranians for 444 days until President Carter was able to negotiate their release.

Meanwhile, in Iraq, the military dictator Saddam Hussein took power. He soon plunged his country into war against neighboring Iran; the conflict over the border between the two countries began in 1980 and lasted eight years. Elsewhere, Lebanon continued to struggle with civil war until Syria sent in troops as peacekeepers. In the West Bank, Palestinians turned to terrorism in their struggle against the Israelis. Indeed, Israel found that its war of occupation in the West Bank was proving to be every bit as bloody as the assaults it had suffered in its four wars against the Arab states.

Death of King Hussein, February 7, 1999

These two Jordanian women are weeping outside of the King Hussein Medical Center in Amman, Jordan, following the death of King Hussein from complications due to cancer at age 63.

7
The Death of Hussein

During the 1970s and 1980s, when much of the Arab world sought to punish Jordan for its refusal to fight in the Yom Kippur War, the one Middle East state that maintained close ties with King Hussein was Iraq.

Hussein's cousins had ruled Iraq since the 1920s, but in 1958 King Faisal and other members of the Hashemite ruling family were murdered in a brutal coup d'etat engineered by Iraqi army General Abdel-Karim Kassem.

Kassem was overthrown five years later. For the next three years a series of military rulers led the government, some of them lasting no more than a few months until they were ousted by ambitious and devious schemers in the Iraqi army. In 1968, a former military leader named Saddam Hussein seized power. Saddam Hussein had been on the losing end of one of the coups of 1963; he fled Iraq that year with a price on his head, but sneaked back into the country five years later and led a successful uprising.

Once in power, Saddam aimed to keep it. He struck back at his enemies with a viciousness and cruelty unusual even by Iraqi standards. He successfully eliminated his enemies, consolidated his power, and ruled Iraq with an iron fist. To secure his rule, Saddam is rumored to have murdered some 17,000 of his political enemies. In February 1992, the United Nations Human Rights Commission issued a report on Iraq that stated "the violations of human rights which have occurred are so grave and are of such a massive nature that since the Second World War few parallels can be found."

Iraq refused to go along with the repudiation of Jordan following the Yom Kippur War. Indeed, the two countries became important trading partners. By the 1980s, the oil-rich Iraqis were pouring $450 million a year into the Jordanian economy. Iraq was the lone Arab nation in the Middle East willing to sell oil to Jordan. When Iraq and Iran went to war in 1980, Jordan supported Iraq. Hussein believed the fundamentalist Islamic revolution that had booted the shah out of power in Iran could spread to other Middle East monarchies, and that the Hashemite sovereignty in Jordan could be in danger. During the eight years of the Iraq–Iran war, Hussein met some 50 times with Saddam in Baghdad, sharing intelligence with the Iraqi leader that the Jordanian military had been able to gather. The two men shared a love for fishing and spent long hours on the Tigris River; after the fishing was over, their families would gather at one of Saddam's palaces, where the two Arab rulers barbecue and dine on the catch of the day.

"When he and I went carp fishing we would talk for hours," King Hussein recalled. "He's very straightforward, very deep and thoughtful, highly intelligent. We would discuss many things—everything."

During those long hours on the Tigris, it is likely that the two leaders shared their disdain for their wealthy Arab neighbors—particularly the Kuwaitis. King Hussein harbored a deep loathing for the Kuwaitis, whom he regarded as cheapskates. When the king had asked Sheikh Sabah, Kuwait's ruler, for $1 million to help fund a university in Jordan, the Kuwaiti had dismissed the request, explaining that a country as poor as Jordan should not be wasting its money on universities.

The Iraq–Iran war had bankrupted Iraq. What's more, in May 1990 the price of oil slumped to $14 a barrel, some $7 less than it had been just six months before. Saddam Hussein was angry at Saudi Arabia and Kuwait, which he claimed were over-producing oil and depressing its price. Saddam had asked Kuwait, which shared a border with Iraq, for $10 billion in economic aid to assist the country until oil prices rose; the parsimonious Kuwaitis had insulted the Iraqi leader by offering just $500 million. Also, the Kuwaitis had refused to forgive billions of dollars in loans they had made to Saddam during his war with Iran.

Saddam had other complaints against the Kuwaitis. The main one involved the Kuwaitis' claim to ownership of two oil-rich islands in the Persian Gulf. During the summer of 1990, tensions between the two countries were strained. On July 30, King Hussein arrived in Baghdad to speak with Saddam, who assured him that he had no intention of attacking the Kuwaitis. The king accepted Saddam's word, then flew on to Kuwait.

King Hussein met with Sheikh Saad, the Kuwaiti crown prince.

"He is very angry with you," Hussein is said to have told Saad.

"But is there a military threat?" the prince asked.

"Oh, no," Hussein answered.

"Then why has he [Saddam] massed troops on our frontier?" Saad demanded to know.

King Hussein returned to Jordan. On July 31, he telephoned President George Bush in Washington and advised him of the military threat posed by Iraq to Kuwait. Two days later, Iraqi troops crossed the border and attacked Kuwait.

The invasion proved to be a disaster for Iraq. The United States mobilized an international coalition which invaded Iraq on January 17, 1991. It was all over in less than 60 days. "Operation Desert Storm" ousted the Iraqis from Kuwait and drove them back to Baghdad, but not before the Iraqis plundered and vandalized Kuwaiti cities and set fire to dozens of oil wells. Bush elected not to pursue the war past the eviction of the Iraqis from Kuwait, a decision America and its Western allies would soon regret as Saddam slowly re-armed his military and backed terrorist groups.

King Hussein remained loyal to Saddam during the Gulf War. He refused to send troops to join the American-led coalition, which angered President Bush. For years, the king had been a welcome visitor to White House parties and other diplomatic functions around Washington, but after the war, Bush remained hostile to the king and he was no longer invited to the American capital. U.S. Secretary of State James Baker called the king's support for Iraq "an act of personal betrayal that had caused the president great personal anguish."

Still, America needed Hussein. That fall, Bush organized a Palestinian-Israeli peace conference in Madrid, Spain. The Israelis were insisting that Palestinians with no links to the PLO be represented at the conference. Baker approached Hussein and asked him to draw up a list of Palestinian leaders who would be acceptable to the Israelis. Hussein, anxious to get back into Washington's good graces, responded quickly to Baker's request. As for Hussein, he went to Madrid with the hope of becoming an influential leader in the talks, but soon found Palestinian leaders taking a hard line toward Israel and unwilling to seek his guidance. The Madrid talks ended with no agreements, but the two sides indicated they'd be willing to pursue further negotiations.

Indeed, the Israelis and the PLO continued to talk. In August 1993, while meeting in Oslo, Norway, the Israelis agreed to turn over Gaza and the city of Jericho on the West Bank to the Palestinians. More significantly, under the Oslo agreement the PLO recognized the Jewish state's right to exist and Israel, in turn, recognized the PLO as the official representative of the Palestinian people. The Israelis also agreed to give Palestinians control over education, taxation, health, tourism, and welfare in the West Bank, but stopped short of granting the PLO total self-government. It was agreed, though, that the two sides would work together to draft a plan that would eventually lead to West Bank independence. The Israeli army would remain in the West Bank and Gaza to protect the Israeli settlements there.

The formal agreement, known as the "Declaration of Principles," was signed on the White House lawn on September 13, 1993.

"You know, we have a lot of work to do," Israeli Prime Minister Yitzhak Rabin told Arafat during the signing of the peace accords.

"I know, and I am prepared to do my part," Arafat answered.

With peace declared between the PLO and Israel, Hussein seized the initiative and proposed his own treaty with the Jewish state. On July 25, 1994, Hussein and Rabin agreed to the terms of a treaty that would open the borders of the two countries. The treaty stated: "Jordan and Israel aim at the achievement of a just, lasting and comprehensive peace. . . . [T]he long conflict between the two states is now coming to an end. . . . [T]he state of belligerency between Jordan and Israel has been terminated."

The treaty, which was formally signed on October 26, 1994, on a strip of desert known as Wadi Arava along the Israeli-Jordanian border, opened border crossings between the two countries, connected Israeli and Jordanian utility lines, opened each other's airports to both Israeli and Jordanian planes, exchanged ambassadors, and ended a trade boycott the two nations had observed against one another for decades.

"It is not only our two states that are making peace with each other today, not only our nations that are shaking hands in Arava," Rabin said. "You and I, Your Majesty, are making peace here, our own peace: the peace of soldiers and the peace of friends."

The Americans were also delighted with the peace initiative. By now, Bill Clinton had replaced Bush as the American president and harbored no hard feelings toward the king. After Jordan and Israel signed the treaty, Clinton traveled to Amman, where he addressed the Jordanian parliament and announced that he would write off Jordan's American debts, provide military aid, and regard Jordan as an ally of the United States.

Alas, Rabin would pay a deep price for his willingness to make peace with the Palestinians and Jordanians. In

Israel, radical Jews still feared the Arab states and opposed any treaties with Arabs. Some Jews turned to terrorism themselves to prevent the establishment of a Palestinian homeland.

On November 4, 1995, Yigal Amir, a 24-year-old Israeli law student, attended a peace rally where Rabin was scheduled to speak. At the rally, Amir drew a 9-mm Beretta handgun and assassinated the prime minister. He was sentenced to life in prison.

Hussein attended the funeral and delivered a eulogy for his friend and former enemy. He said, "I never thought that a moment such as this would come, when I would grieve the loss of a brother, a colleague and a friend, a man, a soldier who met us on the opposite side of the divide, whom we respected as he respected us, a man I came to know because I realized, as he did, that we have to cross over the divide, establish a dialogue, get to know each other and strive to leave for those who follow us a legacy that is worthy of them. And so we did, and so we became brethren and friends."

Jordan's relations with the Israelis remained cordial, but were often strained. After Rabin's death, hard-line Israeli leaders expanded Jewish settlements in the West Bank, angering Hussein as well as Arafat, inasmuch as the Oslo agreement required the Israelis and the newly formed Palestine Authority to be working toward West Bank autonomy. Meanwhile, Palestinian terrorist groups that Arafat found himself unable to control waged attacks on Israeli citizens. The groups, such as Hamas and Islamic Jihad, made use of suicide bombers—known as *shaheed*—to commit terrorism. Israel responded to the attacks with deadly air strikes aimed at terrorist strongholds. By 2002, relations between the Palestinian terrorists and Israelis had degenerated into warfare. To Israelis,

independence for the West Bank had become virtually unthinkable.

❖   ❖   ❖

In 1998, King Hussein started suffering from weight loss, occasional fever, and fatigue. A medical examination uncovered cancer in his lymph glands. In July, the king traveled to the Mayo Clinic in Minnesota to begin chemotherapy. He spent several months in Minnesota, but left the hospital occasionally for diplomatic duties. In October, Hussein made an appearance at the Wye River Plantation near Washington, where President Clinton had been overseeing talks between Arafat and Israeli Prime Minister Benjamin Netanyahu. The world leaders meeting at Wye River couldn't help but notice the king had lost considerable weight and had gone bald from the chemotherapy treatments. Clearly, the king was dying.

In a radio broadcast from the Mayo Clinic beamed back to Jordan, Hussein told his people: "My general condition is excellent, my mind is clear, and my morale is high. This is a new battle among the many battles and, with God's help, we will overcome this problem."

Nevertheless, Hussein did not believe that he would survive his ordeal with cancer, and he took steps to secure his throne's succession.

Since 1965, the crown prince of Jordan had been Hussein's brother Hassan. Over the years, Hassan had never endeared himself to the Jordanian people and often angered Hussein by meddling in the affairs of the army. Hassan was also believed to be cold toward Queen Noor. Before leaving for the Mayo Clinic, Hussein spoke with Hassan, questioning his 51-year-old brother on the role Noor and his children would play in the selection of the crown prince following Hassan's succession to the throne. Hussein specifically asked that a Hashemite family council be established to advise Hassan on the selection, and that one of the king's sons be selected as crown prince. But Hassan insisted such matters could wait until after the king's passing. On January 19, 1999, Hussein returned to Jordan. He had decided that Hassan would not succeed him to the Hashemite throne.

Instead, he named his oldest son Abdullah crown prince. Abdullah, 36, was a career army officer. His mother was Hussein's second wife, an English woman named Toni Gardner whom the king had divorced in 1972. Hard-line Jordanians questioned the selection, inasmuch as Abdullah was half-English. But as a career soldier, Abdullah knew he could count on the unquestioned loyalty of the Jordanian army. What's more, Abdullah was married to Princess Rania, a West Bank Palestinian. Therefore, Palestinians, who still made up half of Jordan's population, could find a reason to support the crown prince.

King Hussein spent just a few days in Jordan before returning to the Mayo Clinic. The king received more chemotherapy treatments, then underwent a bone marrow transplant, which failed to alleviate the cancer. On February 5, the king lost consciousness. He was flown home to Jordan.

On February 7, 1999, after ruling Jordan for 46 years, Hussein bin Talal died. He was 63 years old. The people of Jordan were stricken with grief. Jordanians wept in sorrow and filled mosques to pray for the soul of the dead king. Hundreds of mourners stood in the pouring rain outside the hospital in Amman where the king's body lay. One of those mourners was Mohammed Bahesh, a 24-year-old hotel clerk who had waited for hours in the rain. "Until now, we did not believe that he would die," Bahesh told a newspaper reporter.

In Israel, Jews grieved as well. They had lost their closest friend among the Arab leaders. In 1997, the king had attended a funeral for the Israeli victims of a Jordanian terrorist. The king had kneeled before the family members of the victims, his eyes filled with tears. Miriam Meiri, whose daughter was killed in the attack, recalled, "The king said one sentence I'll never forget: 'I promise you peace.' It gave me the strength to get up the next morning with a smile and tell Yaela, my daughter in heaven: 'There will be peace.'"

The crown prince was declared King Abdullah II two hours after the death of his father. For his part, Abdullah promised to carry on his father's policies, to observe the treaty with Israel, and to continue working for peace in the Middle East. Indeed, one year into his rule, Jordanian police thwarted a terrorist plan to attack United States and Israeli targets; six men were sentenced to death by a Jordanian court.

Years before he died, Hussein was asked by a reporter whether he feared death.

He answered:

I suppose every man is afraid of it up to a certain point; if he weren't, he wouldn't be human. But I am far more afraid of failing to live up to what my people expect of me, those who've always given me their support and who've shared my thoughts, those who have the same clarity of thought regarding the affairs of this part of the world and the future of all of us. I fear what will be said about me years after my death if I don't do everything that must be done at exactly the right time. I face all dangers as dangers to my people, rather than to myself. That is how I've been able to carry out my mission, and that is how, with the help of the divine will, I will continue to do so.

Gallery of Photographs
from Jordan

Gertrude Bell (1868–1926)

Gertrude Bell, an English traveler and explorer and a prolific writer, was instrumental in determining the borders of the new nation of Iraq and in choosing its first ruler, Prince Faisal I (1921). For years, she was his closest personal and political advisor, a position that earned her the title of "Uncrowned Queen of Iraq."

In November 1899, Bell arrived in Jerusalem, the second of her many trips through the Middle East. She immersed herself in studying Arabic. "I am so wildly interested in Arabic that I think of nothing else," she wrote. She watched in amazement as Turkish soldiers kept apart factions willing to fight over every inch of the Holy Land. The rites and rituals of religious pilgrims fascinated her.

In 1900, with the permission of local Turkish authorities, she began an unprecedented trip to ancient ruins within present-day Jordan. These photographs, which Bell donated to the Royal Geographical Society, rank among the earliest of these ancient ruins.

Kharana Castle, 1900

The Kharana Castle is in the desert east of Amman. It was constructed during the late seventh century A.D. by the Umayyads, the first Islamic dynasty. The Umayyads presided over a tremendous expansion of the Muslim world—to North Africa, Spain, and Central Asia.

Kharana is extremely well preserved. It probably was used as a stopover on trade routes between Amman and Damascus, or possibly as a meeting place where local tribal matters and differences could be discussed and settled.

The Graffiti Room, Kharana Castle, 1900

The graffiti room is so called because of a scrawled inscription directly below a small arch over a doorway. Though very faded, it reads: "Abd al-Malik, the son of 'Ubayd, wrote it on Monday three days from Muharram of the year 92" [Muharram is the first month of the Islamic year, so the date would be November 24, 710.] Through the centuries, other graffiti has been placed on the walls of this ornate room with its arcades, rosette friezes, and semidomed ceiling—all visible in this unique photograph, the first of its kind.

Al Qasr, 1900

Al Qasr is between Madaba and al Karak, east of the King's Highway. There are ruins of a first-century B.C. Nabataean temple here. The photograph is of the well-preserved arched cistern opposite the temple entrance.

Ruins of Nabataean Temple, al Qasr, 1900

This first-century B.C. Nabataean temple is thought to have been originally elaborately ornamented. Ancient decorated pieces have been found built into houses of the nearby modern village as well as scattered among the ruins.

Tent of Huwaytat Sheik, 1900

Gertrude Bell encountered several Bedouins on her trip through Jordan. One group, the Beni Sakhr, the last Arab tribe to submit to Ottoman rule, was hostile and most menacing. However, other Bedouins, such as the Huwaytat, whose sheik's tent is shown here, gave Bell and her Turkish-soldier escort complete hospitality.

Women of the Huwaytat Sheik's Harem, 1900

In Muslim countries, a harem is that part of the living quarters set apart for the women of the family.
Gertrude Bell recorded that these Arab women had "their faces tattooed with indigo, their heads and bodies covered in blue cotton gowns." Unveiled and curious, they sold her a hen and some sour milk—yogurt—called *laban*.

Burqu Fort, near Jawa, 1900

Northern Jordan is the location of several archaeological sites that were originally trading towns or security posts in ancient times. This Roman fort was built on a site dating back to the seventh century B.C.

Bethany, c. 1905

Bethany is a small village just outside Jerusalem on the eastern slopes of the Mount of Olives. It is frequently mentioned in the New Testament and is widely visited by Christian pilgrims.

Bethany was under Jordanian control from 1949 until 1967. After the Six-Day War (1967), it became part of the West Bank territory under Israeli administration.

Headquarters, Transjordan Reserve Force, al Karak, 1921

The Transjordan Reserve Force chose the remains of this early-14th-century Mamluke palace as its headquarters in al Karak. Mamlukes were former slaves who were members of a powerful Egyptian military class from about 1250 to 1517 A.D.

On August 21, 1920, Sir Herbert Samuel, the High Commissioner for Palestine, announced that Great Britain supported a separate Transjordan within the British sphere of influence. Almost immediately, Captain C.D. Brunton established a small police force to keep order among the various tribes and to assist in establishing local governments in the towns. Brunton's Transjordan Reserve Force, later the Arab Legion, evolved into today's Jordanian army.

Castle Wall, al Karak, 1921

Al Karak has always been important because of its strategic location at the head of the Wadi al Karak, which leads west to Palestine. (*Wadi* is Arabic for a stream or valley.)

Photographed here is the southwest corner of the castle wall, probably built by the Mamlukes in the early 14th century. The castle dominates the skyline. Today, the Jordanian government is restoring the impressive glacis—that is, the banks of earth in front of the fortification.

Al'Aqaba, c. 1923

The Red Sea is on the left in this photograph, which was taken along the coast looking toward the mountains of the north.

At the beginning of the 20th century, Al'Aqaba was only a small village. Pilgrim traffic through the town to Mecca had disappeared after the opening of the Suez Canal (1869) and the completion of the Hejaz Railroad (1908). T. E. Lawrence ("Lawrence of Arabia") captured Al'Aqaba from the Ottomans in 1917. It became part of the Kingdom of the Hejaz but was ceded to Transjordan in 1924.

Al'Aqaba is Jordan's only outlet to the sea. Today, although its chief importance is as a port, Al'Aqaba is also the nation's only real beach resort.

The Theater, Petra, 1924

This 7000-seat theater was first constructed by the Nabataeans in the early-first century A.D. It was redone by the Romans after their conquest in 106 A.D. Obviously, the Romans did not respect the Nabataean tombs (center of photograph), which they sliced through to expand the theater.

The Deir, c. 1920

The Deir, c. 1920

The Deir is the largest of all Petra's monuments. Some scholars believe that it may have been a temple.

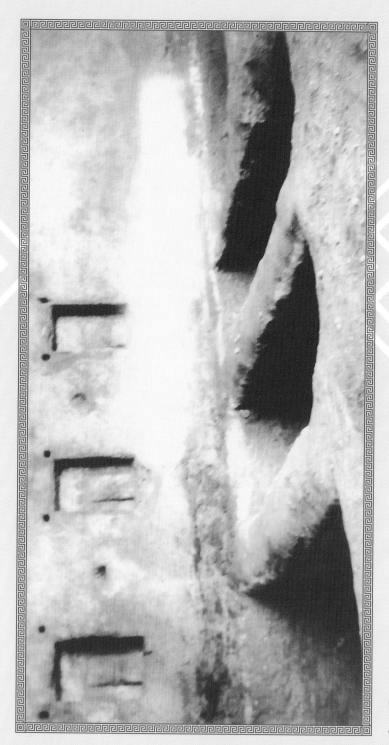

Qasr Burqu, 1929

Qasr Burqu, in the desert east of Amman, is the site of the rarely photographed, long-abandoned Burqu Islamic Palace. The room shown is the longest room and bears several religious inscriptions on the lime-coated walls, dating back to 700 A.D. (upper part of photograph). These Arabic religious inscriptions have dates: 700, 1389, and 1409. The castle may have been built to guard a nearby water supply for passing caravans, although its origins remain uncertain.

Tiers of "Houses," Siyaha/Mount Nebo, 1929

From Amman to Petra, the King's Highway winds past a wealth of historical sites. It is an ancient route that follows the ridge of mountains east of the Dead Sea. This route has been used throughout history by armies, traders, and pilgrims, all of whom have left their mark.

This 1929 photograph is of tiers of "houses" near the Moses Memorial Church at the base of Mount Nebo. Mount Nebo is reputed to be the place from which God showed Moses the Promised Land as well as the site of the death of Moses. For centuries, this area has attracted pilgrims of all faiths who have sought shelter in these "houses." Today, there is a four-star hotel with spa facilities here, allowing the same religious places to be visited in comfort.

Interior of "House," Siyaha/Mount Nebo, 1929

This photograph is from the interior of a "house" at the base of Mount Nebo. Archeological remains found in the rubble left behind by pilgrims date to the sixth century A.D.

Ancient Copper Smelting Pits, Sabra, 1929

The ancient kingdom of Edom, now in southwestern Jordan, was noted for its copper deposits—its most important commodity. Archeologists believe that the copper smelting pits in this photograph were used during the seventh century B.C.

Smelting is the process for obtaining a metal from its ore. Heating to high temperatures cause other substances to burn off. The Edomites probably used charcoal for this purpose.

As-Salt, c. 1924

The ancient agricultural town of as-Salt, in west-central Jordan, is on the old main highway (often called the as-Salt Road) leading from Amman to Jerusalem. The town gave its name to the sultana, a tasty, sweet raisin produced here for centuries.

Improvements on this road were recommended by T. E. Lawrence ("Lawrence of Arabia") during his momentous three-month visit to Amman in 1921. Lawrence's intercessions with the British Foreign Office saved Transjordan for Amir (later King) Abdullah and thus the Hashemite royal house for Jordan.

This photograph was taken by Major Andrew H. Holt, who was assigned to the British legation in Amman. Holt was an expert on field astronomy.

Mamluke Tower, c. 14th Century, as-Salt

This mosque on the citadel hill in as-Salt was the site of a Mamluke castle. The castle tower and the ruins of the walls (both pictured here in this 1924 photograph) no longer exist.

The Mamlukes were armies of former slaves whose generals won political control over Egypt and Syria, 1250–1517. The Mamlukes endowed Cairo with some of its most impressive monuments, many of which are still standing.

3000 B.C.	Nomadic tribes establish settlements along the Jordan River.
About 610 A.D.	The Prophet Muhammad founds Islam.
12th century	Muslim leader Saladin establishes an Arab empire.
16th century	Ottoman Turks rule much of the Middle East.
1916	Great Arab Revolt ousts the Turks from Arab states.
1917	Balfour Declaration commits Great Britain to establishment of a Jewish state in Palestine.
1921	British diplomat Winston Churchill creates the nation of Transjordan out of territory taken from Syria; Hashemite ruler Abdullah is named emir.
1935	Hussein ibn Talal, grandson of Abdullah, born in Amman, Transjordan.
1946	Great Britain grants independence to Transjordan; Abdullah becomes king of the Hashemite Kingdom of Jordan.
1947	United Nations sanctions the creation of a Jewish state in Palestine across the Jordan River.
1948	Israel defeats Arab armies of Iraq, Jordan, Syria, Lebanon, and Egypt to win independence.
1950	Abdullah annexes the West Bank, making the Palestinian homeland a part of Jordan.
1951	Abdullah assassinated; his son, Talal, is briefly king but is removed from office due to mental illness.
1953	Crown Prince Hussein turns 18 and is proclaimed king.
1956	Hussein dismisses John Bagot Glubb as head of the Arab Legion, ending British control over the Jordanian military.
1958	Egypt and Syria form the United Arab Republic, threatening the autonomy of Jordan.
1964	Arab states recognize establishment of Palestine Liberation Organization; terrorist attacks begin on Israel.
1967	Jordan, Syria and Egypt lose territory to Israel as a result of the Six-Day War.
1968	Armed Palestinian fighters battle Israeli troops in the Jordan village of Karameh.
1969	Yasir Arafat named PLO chairman.

1970 Hussein fights off a Syrian invasion and puts down a Palestinian uprising, then drives Palestinians out of his country; within a year, some 4,000 Palestinians would be killed by Jordanian soldiers.

1971 Jordanian Prime Minister Wasfi al-Tall assassinated by the Palestinian group Black September.

1972 Black September terrorists murder nine Israeli athletes and two other people at the Munich Olympics.

1973 Egypt and Syria attack Israel in the Yom Kippur War, but the aggressors are driven back.

1974 Arab leaders strip Jordan of its responsibility for the Palestinians, recognizing the PLO as the sole legitimate representatives of the Palestinian people.

1988 Jordan renounces claims to the West Bank.

1991 Jordan supports Iraq in the Persian Gulf War.

1994 Jordan signs a peace treaty with Israel.

1999 King Hussein dies of cancer; his son, Crown Prince Abdullah, is proclaimed new king of Jordan.

Abdullah of Jordan. *My Memoirs Completed*. Translated by Harold W. Glidden. London: Longman, 1978.

Dallas, Roland. *King Hussein: A Life on the Edge*. New York: Fromm International, 1999.

Field, Michael. *Inside the Arab World*. Cambridge, Mass.: Harvard University Press, 1994.

Gilbert, Martin. *Winston Churchill*. Boston, Mass.: Houghton Mifflin Co., 1975.

Hussein of Jordan. *Uneasy Lies the Head*. London: Heinemann, 1962.

James, Lawrence. *The Golden Warrior: The Life and Legend of Lawrence of Arabia*. New York: Paragon House, 1993.

Lawrence, T. E. *Seven Pillars of Wisdom*. New York: Penguin Books, 1962.

Lunt, James. *Hussein of Jordan*. New York: William Morrow and Co., 1989.

Markarian, Zohrab. *King and Country*. London: Hutchinson Benham, 1986.

Miller, Judith. *God Has Ninety-Nine Names*. New York: Touchstone, 1997.

Nash, Jay Robert. *Terrorism in the 20th Century*. New York: M. Evans and Co., 1998.

Reeve, Simon. *One Day in September*. New York: Arcade Publishing, 2000.

Salibi, Kamal. *The Modern History of Jordan*. New York: I.B. Tauris, 1993.

Sparrow, Gerald. *Hussein of Jordan*. London: George G. Harrap and Co., 1960.

Wilson, Mary C. *King Abdullah, Britain and the Making of Jordan*. Cambridge, England: Cambridge University Press, 1987.

Yardley, Michael. *T. E. Lawrence: A Biography*. New York: Stein and Day, 1987.

Broder, John H. "Clinton Gives Condolences and a Pledge of Support." *The New York Times,* Feb. 8, 1999.

Dallas, Roland. *King Hussein: A Life on the Edge.* New York: Fromm International, 1999.

Field, Michael. *Inside the Arab World.* Cambridge, Mass.: Harvard University Press, 1994.

Friedman, Thomas L. "King Hussein, 1935-1999." *The New York Times,* Feb. 8, 1999.

Friedman, Thomas. "Rabin and Arafat Seal Their Accord as Clinton Applauds 'Brave Gamble.'" *The New York Times,* Sept. 14, 1993.

Gilbert, Martin. *Winston Churchill Volume IV: 1916-1922.* Boston, Mass.: Houghton Mifflin Co., 1975.

Hussein of Jordan. "Holy Land, My Country." *National Geographic,* December 1964.

Jehl, Douglas. "Hussein of Jordan, Voice for Peace, Dies." *The New York Times,* Feb. 8, 1999.

Jehl, Douglas. "Once Derided, Noor is Likely to Remain a Power at the Palace." *The New York Times,* Feb. 8, 1999.

James, Lawrence. *The Golden Warrior: The Life and Legend of Lawrence of Arabia.* New York: Paragon House, 1993.

Lawrence, T. E. *Seven Pillars of Wisdom.* New York: Penguin Books, 1962.

Leprince, V. "Conversation with King Hussein." *Oui,* January 1973.

Lunt, James. *Hussein of Jordan.* New York: William Morrow and Co., 1989.

Marden, Luis. "The Other Side of Jordan." *National Geographic,* December 1964.

Miller, Judith. "Cautious King Took Risks In Straddling Two Worlds." *The New York Times,* Feb. 8, 1999.

Miller, Judith. *God Has Ninety-Nine Names.* New York: Touchstone, 1997.

Nash, Jay Robert. *Terrorism in the 20th Century.* New York: M. Evans and Co., 1998.

Orme, William A. Jr. "Abullah II: A Military Man and Now Jordan's New Ruler." *The New York Times,* Feb. 8, 1999.

Reeve, Simon. *One Day in September.* New York: Arcade Publishing, 2000.

Salibi, Kamal. *The Modern History of Jordan.* New York: I. B. Tauris, 1993.

Sontag, Deborah. "Outpouring of Israeli Grief, and Wariness for the Future."
The New York Times, Feb. 8, 1999.

Yardley, Michael. *T. E. Lawrence: A Biography.* New York: Stein and Day, 1987.

"Arab Decepta: A People Self-Deluded." *Time,* July 14, 1967.

"The Boy King." *Time,* April 2, 1956.

"The Least Unreasonable Arab." *Time,* July 14, 1967.

"New Crown Prince: 'Extension of Old King.'" Reuters, Feb. 8, 1999.

WEB SITE SOURCES:

The 1948 War of Independence
Jewish Virtual Library
http://www.us-israel.org/jsource/History/1948toc.html

De Havilland Dove
http://users.chariot.net.au/~theburfs/doveMAIN.html

Hashemite Kingdom of Jordan
http://www.kinghussein.gov.jo

History of Jordan
http://www.kingabdullah.jo

Embassy of Jordan
http://www.jordanembassyus.org

NewsHour Interview with King Hussein
http://www.pbs.org/newshour/bb/middle_east/october96/hussein_10-3.html

Royalty in Jordan
http://www.royalty.nu/MiddleEast/Jordan/Hussein.html

Cover: Royal Geographical Society

Frontispiece: Royal Geographical Society

page:

18: AP/Wide World Photos

21: © Hulton-Deutsch Collection/Corbis

54: Hulton Archive by Getty Images

57: AP/Wide World Photos

64: AP/Wide World Photos

83: Hulton Archive by Getty Images

87: © Bettmann/Corbis

95: AP/Wide World Photos

97: AP/Wide World Photos

100: © AFP/Corbis

104: AP/Wide World Photos

Unless otherwise credited all photographs in this book © Royal Geographical Society.
No reproduction of images without permission.
Royal Geographical Society
1 Kensington Gore
London SW7 2AR

Unless otherwise credited the photographs in this book are from the Royal Geographical
Society Picture Library. Most are being published for the first time.

The Royal Geographical Society Picture Library provides an unrivaled source of over
half a million images of the peoples and landscapes from around the globe. Photographs
date from the 1840s onwards on a variety of subjects including the British Colonial Empire,
deserts, exploration, indigenous peoples, landscapes, remote destinations, and travel.

Photography, beginning with the daguerreotype in 1839, is only marginally younger
than the Society, which encouraged its explorers to use the new medium from its earliest
days. From the remarkable mid-19th century black-and-white photographs to color trans-
parencies of the late 20th century, the focus of the collection is not the generic stock shot
but the portrayal of man's resilience, adaptability and mobility in remote parts of the world.

In organizing this project, we have incurred many debts of gratitude. Our first,
though, is to the professional staff of the Picture Library for their generous assistance,
especially to Joanna Wright, Picture Library Manager.

HAL MARCOVITZ is a journalist for *The Morning Call*, a newspaper based in Allentown, Pennsylvania. He has written more than 30 books for young readers, including biographies of Robin Williams, Ron Howard, Al Sharpton, and Don King for Chelsea House. He lives in Chalfont, Pennsylvania, with his wife, Gail, and daughters Ashley and Michelle.

AKBAR S. AHMED holds the Ibn Khaldun Chair of Islamic Studies at the School of International Service of American University. He is actively involved in the study of global Islam and its impact on contemporary society. He is the author of many books on contemporary Islam, including *Discovering Islam: Making Sense of Muslim History and Society,* which was the basis for a six-part television program produced by the BBC called *Living Islam.* Ahmed has been a visiting professor and the Stewart Fellow in the Humanities at Princeton University, as well as a visiting professor at Harvard University and Cambridge University.